Disrupting Systemic Cycles of Faulty Thinking

As I **THINK** I Become
As I **SPEAK** I Create
I **DO** the Work

CHARMAS B. LEE and JANICE K. LEE
PATRICIA L. DENNARD, CONTRIBUTING AUTHOR

Also by Charmas and Janice Lee

Hiding in Plain Sight

A Different Kind of Champion

Run Your Race

Stay in Your Lane

Resisting Success

First Edition

Library of Congress Control Number: 2019904532
ISBN: 978-1094901039

To Calvin

This book is dedicated to those who possess one of the greatest ambitions of all; to cultivate, nurture and develop the minds of our future.
Go Wolfpack!

Make each day a glorified exhibition of brilliance

[signature]
Jamaal R Lee

Charmas Lee is the "real deal" and his *Think Say Do* approach to creating champions, in all walks of life, is something we all need. He ignites the heart and influences the mind of every life he touches.

Beth V. Walker
Founder, Center for College Solutions

Most of us have heard that performance is 95% physiological and 5% psychological; but Charmas Lee says, "What most of us do not understand is that the 5% psychological, rules the 95% physiological." I was hooked after reading that. This is so true not only in sports, but in relationships! Having competed against Olympic basketball players and now coaching people in interpersonal and business relationships, I found the insights in *Think Say Do* to be encouraging, inspiring, challenging and obtainable! I wished I had these principles as a player. In coaching successful relationships, Charmas Lee's insights are invaluable because they work! This book is a slam dunk!

-- Dr. Clarence Shuler, President/CEO
BLR: Building Lasting Relationships

Coach Charmas Lee gets a first-round knock-out with his new book *Think Say Do*. Coach Charmas uses real life situations and gives us real solutions to help solve social challenges that we face as a society. As a coach myself the mindset an individual has when they encounter or get put in difficult situations is the key to solving or overcoming a problem. Think Say Do is now an essential tool for my toolbox for me to reference during my coaching endeavors!

-- Jamie Belt CSCS, RSCC, CES
Professional Strength Coach

Think Say Do is far and away a potent and useful approach for any organization, entrepreneur, or leader to implement. The content is bulletproof! A must read.

-- Joe Aldaz, Program Manager,
Institute for Veterans and Military Families

When Charmas Lee speaks, I listen; when he writes, I read. This is not only so because Coach Lee is a uniquely gifted communicator but because his walk matches his talk. He is a humble and teachable man. These are attributes of his character – God molded. His gift of leading others is a manifestation of his life choices and his desire to have people experience their God-given purposes in life.

-- Tim DeVore, Management Coach
DeVore Incorporated

I have been an educator and coach for over 29 years and have seen much of what Charmas shares. I find his *Think Say Do* concept very interesting, it hits many truths. Imagine, a society with more self-confidence, more common since, a positive attitude and the desire to achieve something it can be proud of! Having a system like this, that can be taught in patterns, and used in more areas in life than athletics, is something that is needed and would be useful for all ages.

-- Matt Krich
Educator and Coach

FOREWORD

Do you feel that your potential has not quite been met, or that your focus is a little blurred? Are you feeling a little lost in the shuffle of life and in spite of all your efforts, you can't quite get over the hump? Maybe you're a coach, an educator, or a parent who is looking to grow an athlete, student, or child? Are you coachable? If so, *Think Say Do* is for you.

My name is Nate Hansen and during my 18-year professional career in public education, I have served as a teacher, coach, and administrator. As the principal of an Elementary School I work with all types of students and the adults in their lives. I see first-hand the challenges our students and their families face. I work with teachers to help navigate the layers of trauma that they must work through in their classrooms before students can focus on content, and we witness daily the negative impact of a student's lack of ability to problem solve or deal with conflict effectively. These deficits, combined with a sense of learned helplessness have a domino effect on our classrooms, teachers, and ultimately our community and its future. Without specific strategies, continuous practice, and a consistent mantra of positive self-talk, students will continue to struggle with goal setting, and ultimately achieving success. They will continue to be impacted by their own traumas and will continue to be hijacked by their emotions. In his book, *Think Say Do*, Charmas identifies strategies and provides the inspiration and hope for anyone who is seeking better outcomes in their personal and professional life.

Charmas has dedicated his life to motivating, inspiring, and helping people find the best version of themselves. In *Think Say Do* Charmas attempts to enlighten, inspire, and effect the change we all want to see in ourselves and in this country. Charmas offers up some of the techniques, methodologies and stepwise approaches based on the latest information in neuroscience and the 5/95 rule of human performance. These are all techniques that he successfully uses in the athletic, academic and corporate arenas.

I have witnessed the impact Charmas's passion, faith, and techniques can have on people. In the fall of 2018 Charmas began his ACE Project at my school, along with the practices found in **Think Say Do**. The students who have participated in this program have transformed from disengaged students, fighting amongst themselves, to students who are reflective of their choices and the impact of those choices. With the intense pressures that today's youth face, I have no doubt all kids (and adults) need the opportunity to gain greater self-confidence, perseverance, and focus. The practices brought forward in **Think Say Do** have been life-changing for our students and I have committed myself, as a principal, to expose as many of our students to these practices and philosophies as possible. I am certain that the strategies in this book will positively reshape the student culture at my school, and will continue to positively influence these students throughout their lives.

As you will learn from this book, with the right tools and strategies we are all champions.

Nate Hansen
School Administrator, Former Coach, Husband, & Father

AUTHOR'S NOTE

Back in 2015 I was invited to speak at a TEDx event. The title of my message was "The Mind is the Battlefield." During my 18-minute message I introduced the *Think Say Do* model to those in attendance. The message was a success and a new platform was birthed.

Think Say Do is a 3-step process that occurs in a microsecond.
- As I THINK I become
- As I SPEAK (SAY) I create
- I DO the work

The visual image of the yield sign with the words *think say do* serves as a prompt and behavior trigger. We make hundreds of micro-pivots daily to adapt our thinking in an effort to achieve positive outcomes.

The ultimate goal in writing this book is to assist in changing the trajectory of the challenges our country is faced with today and offer insight to those who are seeking better outcomes in life. Our landscape is colored with *unrealized potential*. Decision fatigue and information overload are two examples of the challenges many of us face on a daily basis. From an individual perspective, it is demanding. It is even more taxing from a leadership perspective, where you are not just responsible for yourself. You have to inspire the ones around you to follow your example as well. The concepts, ideas and strategies shared in *Think Say Do* can have demonstratable applications in the academic, athletic and corporate environments.

It addresses the *social competencies* necessary for individuals to succeed. No longer is it just content knowledge that makes people successful in life and the pursuit of goals, but it is the ability to focus, collaborate with others, manage stress and master self-regulation in difficult situations.

If you are striving to rise to the level of your potential and not live at the level of your disappointment, **Think Say Do** is for you. This is about self-discovery, personal mastery, developing a strong mental model, recognizing performance barriers and making a commitment to excellence!

One final note about **Think Say Do** and the many examples used in this book. While I reference students, athletes and educators in many of the scenarios presented, the strategies, concepts, ideas and principles are applicable in all environments for all individuals desiring to disrupt faulty thinking and achieve unparalleled levels of success.

TABLE OF CONTENTS

Introduction

I was scheduled to speak at a conference in beautiful Colorado Springs, Colorado and was going through my pre-presentation routine in my mind. "Good afternoon, welcome to the ABC's of High-Performance Teams! My name is Charmas Lee and I build champions." This was the first of two back-to-back 90-minute break-out sessions designed to improve human productivity. It was the final day of the two-day conference and it was easy to see that many in the audience had reached information overload. To make matters worse it was right after lunch and many were also experiencing the consequences of poor nutritional choices. Many others were physically present, but for whatever reason they were disengaged. Perhaps they were exhausted and simply ready for the conference to end. Which is reasonable, after all it had been two days. Two days of talking, listening and taking notes. I speculate that this group was experiencing the side effects of dehydration, information overload and decision fatigue, which is a recipe for disaster.

Dehydration

The effects of dehydration are pretty serious and can promote a decrease in focus and concentration, confusion (lack of clarity) and an increase of the heart rate by up to 10%. At 6,000 feet above sea level, you perspire and exhale twice the amount of moisture you would at sea level! With an elevation of 6,035 feet Colorado Springs is over a mile above sea level.

Information Overload

Everyone's capacity for information is different. Once we reach information overload comprehension and our ability to make quality decisions is diminished.

Decision Fatigue

You can't make decision after decision without paying a biological price. It's different from ordinary physical fatigue — you're not *consciously aware* of being tired — but you're low on mental energy. The more choices you make throughout the day, the harder each one becomes for your brain. Decision fatigue also makes it a bit more difficult to regulate emotion.

I was really excited about this speaking engagement. As a human performance specialist I knew that if those in the audience could pay attention, prioritize listening and follow through with the instructions, the outcomes could be life changing. Feeling their pain, I announced to the group that "time does not permit me to dive deep into the principles and frameworks I had planned for this afternoon's session. With your permission I'd like to take you beyond the X's and O's in the form of a coaching session and help you warm up your imaginations, give wings to your dreams, bring your personal and professional prowess to life and encourage you to operate at the outer limits of your potential."

By the nodding of heads and a few "go for its" the audience gave me permission to switch things up. I looked out the window and witnessed the beauty of the majestic front range and that is when it hit me. I said to the audience (in my outside coaching voice) "are you coachable?" and I received a resounding yes! There was a park adjacent to the hotel, so I asked the facilitator to grab as much water as possible and meet me and "my team" at the park. Upon arriving at our destination everyone was given a 20-ounce bottle of water and I performed a toast. With water bottles held high I said " Hello champions, welcome to the great outdoors. When is the last time you were called a champion at 1:15 in the afternoon?" The group looked stunned. "I have been a coach for over 31 years, and I can spot a champion or a chump from at least 400 meters away. There is no doubt that you are champions, because you cannot be a coward and be in your profession…cheers to you!"

Increasing Serotonin Levels

We began the outdoor session with something you might hear a team chant at a sporting event. Research has shown that to increase serotonin levels a positive experience must be held in the brain for at least 12 seconds. So I cued up the group and said, "When I say who's great? You say we are." This went on for about 30 seconds. Each time we got louder and louder. Everyone appeared to be having a great time. I spent the next 20 minutes instructing the group on neuromuscular, kinesthetic awareness, proprioception and cross lateral drills. These movement patterns are designed to solicit several different responses from the body both physiologically and psychologically and are used in our athletic program. Cross laterals force both brain hemispheres to "talk" to each other. Kinesthetic awareness supports proprioception. Proprioception is very important to the brain as it plays a big role in self-regulation, coordination, posture, body awareness, and the ability to attend, focus and speak.

I was fortunate enough to have a young lady in the audience who was a former athlete. I was able to use her as a model to demonstrate the drills to the rest of the group. I must confess that watching this group of folks trying to do windmills, cross laterals, shake ups, straight leg bounds, and single leg gallops was amusing, but the key is that they had a ton of fun. They looked like cartoon characters! When we returned to the conference room there was laughter, excitement and the group was fully engaged. It was also a bit sweaty. I guess that is the price you pay when you have adults regressing back to their youth in a constructive manner. This same group of people who had previously been disengaged had become fully engaged and were now *dynamically present.*

Fluid Intelligence

Before I started the presentation, I guided the group through an exercise to improve fluid intelligence. Fluid intelligence is a complex human ability that allows us to adapt our thinking to a new cognitive problem or situation. Fluid intelligence is considered one of the most important factors in learning, and is closely related to professional and educational success especially in complex and demanding environments. I call this exercise pulsing. Pulsing is designed to provide a sense of well-being, remove attention residue and increase the ability to attune to the information shared.

The former group had given me a front row seat to some of the challenges our teachers, employers, coaches, pastors, parents and others in leadership were currently experiencing. The latter group gave me a fresh new perspective on how things can be if we are willing to "unfollow the rules" a bit and move away from some of our traditional models. I also realized how "coaching" versus presenting can make a significant difference when it comes to taking people from inspirational to operational. The emotional state that you feel when learning can determine whether it is stored in the long-term memory or not.

In 2017 I presented/coached one hundred and twelve times within a 9-week time frame using a similar style of coaching, and almost every time the outcome was spectacular. As someone who is looking for ways to inspire positive outcomes, I went on a quest to find the *secret sauce*!

Listed below are the Critical Control Points (CCP's) I've learned to ask myself prior to and during a speaking engagement.

1. How am I showing up?
2. How is my audience (employee, student, spouse etc.) showing up?
3. What state of readiness are they in?
4. Is information overload or decision fatigue a factor?
5. How can I "sell them on themselves?"
6. How can I increase serotonin levels?
7. How can I enhance the re-entry (transition) process and decrease attention residue?

In summary, the lesson you prepare, the lesson you share vs. the lesson they hear is based on the listener's state of readiness.

To be successful it will take endurance, courage, determination, mental tenacity and the willingness to embrace a new thought process while developing the champion that lives within you. Over the last 20 years someone has capitalized on the idea that working hard to achieve what you want to accomplish in life is not required. Stop drinking the Kool-Aid. This is nonsense. If you have bought into this type of thinking and are "waiting for your ship to come in" you have a long wait ahead of you. Stop exchanging an _intellectual argument_ for the truth.

The truth is no great innovation or human leap forward came from a predictable path or an idea that was immediately attainable or realistic. It required hard work. We are responsible for our reality. Decide what you want of the world and go make it happen. We have all heard that rules are made to govern the masses. But those folks who are effecting change in this world simply don't (follow the rules). Don't get me wrong, yes, it is important to follow rules that help protect us and govern society, however when it comes to the way we think it is a different story. Take a look at each accomplishment below. At some point these things were un-thinkable. In each case, someone had to color outside the lines, think outside the box or whatever else you want to call it.

- landing on the moon
- cell phone
- stem cell treatments
- computer

The great say reality can be shaped and changed by direct actions, so they act with constancy to forge an ideal life. They believe actionable dreams have more weight than current circumstances. This requires creativity, imagination, disciplined learning and initiative. In essence our perception is our reality.

The Challenge

Either by choice, circumstance, or both many have lost their "sense of self" which has created a debilitating discouragement. The results are self-evident and have become catastrophic resulting in insecurity, self-doubt, fear, condemnation, behavioral challenges and even lower academic achievement. Suicide rates are skyrocketing, chronic diseases such as heart disease, diabetes, high blood pressure, arteriosclerosis, atherosclerosis and obesity have a stranglehold on our country.

And then there is adrenaline dominance. We know what a surge of adrenaline feels like. It is the hormone that gives us the strength for "fight or flight." Our hearts beat harder, stronger and faster. Blood is diverted from less important things, like digestion, to our muscular tissue. Thought processes seem to happen at lightning speed. There are many stories of superhuman feats performed under extraordinary circumstances with surges of adrenaline. It starts to get "bad" when adrenaline output is too generous, and this type of stress becomes chronic. Our bodies don't have the ability to moderate the high adrenaline.

According to the American Psychological Association, chronic stress is linked to the six leading causes of death: heart disease, cancer, lung ailments, accidents, cirrhosis of the liver and suicide. More than 75 percent of all physician office visits are for stress-related ailments and complaints. Chronic stress can affect your brain, suppress your thyroid, cause blood sugar imbalances, decrease bone density and muscle tissue, raise blood pressure, reduce your immunity and ability to heal, and increase fat deposits around your abdomen that are associated with heart attacks, strokes and elevated "bad" cholesterol. Many experts indicate that stress, anxiety, feelings of poor self-worth and a sense of helplessness may be a bigger contributor to these chronic diseases than pre-disposed genetics or nutrition.

Over the last thirty years I have had hundreds, if not thousands of conversations with those who expressed a *feeling of aimlessness*, eluding to being trapped in a *mental wilderness*. A long-time friend and coaching colleague shared with me that just five years ago he believed that coaching was the greatest profession in the world. In December of 2018 I accompanied him to the athletic director's office where he stated that he was "*tired of doing the impossible for the ungrateful*" and turned in his letter of resignation.

With over 3.6 million teachers nationally as of 2015, more than one out of every 100 Americans is a k-12 educator. Education is going through a turbulent time of change with increased federal regulations, funding shortages and declining enrollments creating a situation of uncertainty. Educators have shared that in growing numbers, students are showing up to the classroom disengaged and distracted, which has increased the potential for crisis and greatly diminished the chances for optimal outcome. The pendulum swings from an inflated sense of entitlement mindset to a poor me defeatist attitude. For some it is the achievement trap and for others it is a learned helplessness.

The American workforce has more than 100 million full-time employees. One-third of those employees are what Gallup refers to as "engaged at work." They love their jobs and make their organization and America better every day. At the other end of the spectrum, 16% of employees are actively disengaged — they are miserable in the workplace and destroy what the most engaged employees build. The remaining 51% of employees are not engaged, they're just there. Both content knowledge and social intelligence are necessary to be successful in the work environment. People are expected to offer innovative ideas in a collaborative environment where they are perceived as competent and dedicated, but yet, not too bossy or pushy. These soft interpersonal skills are not easily mastered and have to be directly taught many times. They are not innate skills.

Americans are faced with a myriad of challenges. The obstacles faced by the young and the old, affluent and impoverished, are overwhelming. Everyone is dealing with a challenge. We are a microcosm of the world. It is human nature to become disillusioned when we are faced with constant challenge. Even the battle tested warrior can fall prey to the stress of being in the trenches day after day and year after year. Nonetheless I encourage you to hold fast to the non-negotiable facts of faith and eternal truth that you are a CHAMPION. With your permission I'd like to coach you on a journey of self-discovery, restore your passion and enthusiasm, give wings to your dreams and bring your personal and professional prowess to life. In order to achieve success however, you will have to be coachable ☺

Success is a journey not a destination, however the journey is much more enjoyable and fulfilling when you set and achieve the proper benchmarks or process goals along the way. The late great John Wooden said, "Success is peace of mind which is a direct result of self-satisfaction in knowing you made the **best** effort to become the **best** of which you are capable." Applying the principles found in *Think Say Do* is an opportunity for you to say no to the status quo where mediocrity lives and say yes to success, and reach for the stars where those who dare to dream and *do the work* reside.

The dream that has been placed inside of you is free, but to see it come to pass you'll have a price to pay. There is no success without risk of failure, no reward without hard work, no opportunity without criticism, and no true success without belief in your own ability. Consistency separates the winners from the wannabees. Diligence makes the difference between the all-time greats and the one-hit wonders. It is time to…

- **Fix your focus**
- **Awaken your courage**
- **Stir your confidence**

5/95 Rule of Human Performance

In the world of high performance there is a rule called the "5/95 rule of human performance" that suggests performance is 95% physiological and 5% psychological, however the 5% controls the 95%. I have modified this rule and developed a stepwise approach to winning in life called *Think Say Do.*

Think Say Do is a *high-performance mental mastery model* that integrates the 5/95 rule of human performance with some of the latest findings in neuroscience. It has been said, "The mind is a magnificent servant but a horrible master." This line of thinking is not new. I have worked with thousands of individuals in the athletic, academic and corporate arena competing in the metaphorical race of life who can't seem to get out of their own way and be at their best when their best is necessary. They have trained, studied or practiced for hundreds of hours only to balk when it is time for the recital, race or the test.

Think Say Do teaches you to analyze situations in real time, helping you make the best decision in the moment. Our approach creates a winning attitude, which is a prerequisite to developing an individual's potential and confidence, building better cultures, stronger communities, careers and outcomes.

Think Say Do hones in on building essential skills; a process through which the user can develop a cognitive strategic plan that breaks larger issues into smaller more manageable ones.

Think Say Do focuses on essential adaptive skills important to academic, business and social success.

Think Say Do addresses both problem solving skills and cognitive flexibility skills essential to overcoming impediments and success in the 21st century.

Every action is preceded by a thought. Our actions may be no wiser than our thoughts, our thinking no greater than our understanding. We can assign a value to every thought. The outcome of any life situation, regardless of how it may be perceived, is neutral. We are able to determine whether it is positive or negative, good or bad, helpful or hurtful. We have all lived long enough to know we can't always control the variables; however we can control how we respond.

Essential Adaptive Skills Important For Success

Developing the Proper Framework for Decision Making

In the early part of the season our athletes undergo a decision making bootcamp. We develop scenarios that can, and potentially will happen throughout the season. I call this *artificial adversity* training. The scenarios reflect various dimensions of their personal, academic and family life and are not just limited to what may occur at practice or in a competition. In essence we teach/train them how to solve problems, with the hope and expectation they will make the best decision in the moment. Being self-confident and able to make decisions for themselves, about themselves and, above all, by themselves are skills that, once developed are incredibly empowering.

Problem Solving/Decision Making Process

There is a difference between solving a problem and making a decision. I have found that many people jump to a conclusion and make a poor decision simply because they don't understand what's required to solve a problem.

Step 1. Identify the problem(s)
Step 2. Identify Facts and Assumptions
Step 3. Generate Alternatives
Step 4. Analyze Alternatives
Step 5. Compare Alternatives
Step 6. Make and Execute Your Decision
Step 7. Assess the Results

While coaching a classroom of 3rd, 4th and 5th graders on the problem solving/decision making process, two young boys began to argue, and a fight almost broke out. Both boys with the group watching, listening and contributing went through the process in "real time." Once we had completed the process the instigator was directed to make and execute his decision. He said now I am going to get him! I share this story with you because many don't possess the proper framework for decision making, however through repetition it will happen. Competence breeds confidence!

Teaching Presence

"*Movement is a language (Presence). If you want them present, teach them presence*☺ "   Charmas B. Lee

We teach students and clients to move with definiteness of purpose. This includes cueing, phrasing and postural alignment. I have heard some of our students call this movement pattern "swag." It is basically a shoulders square, hips tall posture. This is important to the athlete's psychology and sends a message to the competition, "the race is for second." I call it upper- and lower-unit organization. We train them to be organized *intraphysically*. The cue is "you are always on audition." We teach *phrasing* (combinations of *postural alignments* and gestures). For example, you will never see our athletes with their hands on the hips. It communicates the wrong message. The great communicators (verbal and non-verbal) are those who match their phrasing with their communication intentions. This is a great mastery tool for the athlete to also understand what the competitor is thinking.

I am an assistant sprint coach at a local high school. Some of the athletes who attend this high school are also part of the SPEED T&F program of which I am the Executive Director. We have implemented the nuts and bolts from the SPEED system into the high school program including our mental mantra and neuromuscular integration (NI) routine. Recently at a competition, the team had just completed their routine. Our head coach, Ms. King, collected the athletes after the tune-up and asked them an interesting question. "Did you notice how those teams were watching you guys perform your drills and build ups?" The way they perform the routine and move with purpose and intention had affected the psychology of the competition. The comment from the head coach boosted our team's confidence and put the other teams on notice.

Mental Physiology

"We don't come to defend, we come to conquer" is the team's mindset. This may sound a bit aggressive so permit me to explain. We talked about intraphysics earlier and how it relates to movement. It is an inside out approach. "*We don't come to defend, we come to conquer*" is how our *mental physiology* expresses itself and is aimed, not toward the competition, but towards the track, football field, tennis court, classroom, etc. Developing the proper *mental physiology* makes you the weapon and the warrior.

Section One

"Between **stimulus** and **response** there is **space.** In that space lies our power to choose our response. In our response lies our growth and our freedom."

~Victor Frankl, Holocaust Survivor/Austrian Neurologist

We Are What We Think

We are what we think. Psychologist Archibald Hart writes; "Research has shown that one's thought life influences every aspect of one's being." Whether we are filled with confidence or fear depends on the kind of thoughts that *habitually* occupy our minds. According to our friend Mel Robbins, author of the *5 Second Rule;* "There is a 5 second window where the brain moves from idea to action or sabotage sets in." Confusion will lend itself to doubt. Doubt gives rise to the thoughts and feelings of panic and anxiety. Thoughts lead to feelings, feelings lead to actions, actions lead to results. Everything about us *flows* out of the way we think.

- The way we think creates our attitudes.
- The way we think shapes our emotions.
- The way we think governs our behavior.
- The way we think deeply influences our immune system and vulnerability to illness.

Each day many of us are involved in a civil war. It is a war that takes place in our mind and therefore the mind is the battlefield. At any given moment we are either selling ourselves on ourselves or selling ourselves out. It is important to make good thinking a habit. In order to do this we must live each moment in conscious awareness (metacognition).

From the perspective of **emotional intelligence,** administering the ***Think Say Do*** high-performance mental mastery model, **in a moment of crisis or challenge,** teaches us to pause, reflect and not give in to impulsivity, confusion, overwhelming anxiety or a defeatist attitude. Remember Victor Frankl's quote,

"Between stimulus and response there is space. In that space is our power to choose our response. In our response lies our growth and our freedom."

Inner Excellence

Every champion hears two competing voices. One is the negative critic and the other is a positive coach. Which voice we listen to is a matter of choice. Inner excellence is a way of thinking and a way of acting. It is a quality of mind, a mentality that says no matter how difficult things become, we are responsible and accountable for our thoughts, feelings, and actions.

Inner excellence means staying positive in negative situations, not getting hijacked by emotions and learning to deal with adversity in an optimistic way. It is finding love and joy in what you do and remaining steadfastly committed to your goals, values, and dreams. Inner excellence teaches you to stay cool when the heat is on. When you learn to shut off outside influences and believe in yourself there is no telling how great you can be. Belief drives behaviors and self-limiting beliefs lead to self-defeating behaviors.

> "Belief drives behaviors and self-limiting beliefs lead to self-defeating behaviors."

People with inner excellence see challenge from a different perspective. They are motivated by a desire to succeed rather than by a fear of failure. When we possess inner excellence, other people's opinions of us don't matter. We live with a powerful belief in ourselves that is uncommon to others (and in some cases makes others uncomfortable). We have learned to work without applause and believe strongly that every experience in life, whether it be good or bad, has provided us with a form of currency called equity and will reap dividends at the appropriate time.

Learning to Think

Learning to think and use our mind correctly is not only the hardest step, but the first and most powerful step. We can teach ourselves through conscious effort, to gain control of our thoughts and feelings, and in doing so change the programming and chemistry in our brains. What we are thinking every moment of the day becomes a physical reality in the brain and body, effecting our physical and mental health. These thoughts collectively form our attitude which is our state of mind...and it's our **attitude,** not our DNA, that determines much of the quality of our life. Before we begin this process we must learn to suspend disbelief. To suspend disbelief you must first learn to warm up your imagination and clean up your thought life.

Not long ago most athletes believed that hours and hours of conditioning, strength training and other types of practice and physical training were the only things necessary to achieve optimal performance. They thought that only when the body was honed to a peak physiological condition, they'd *feel* ready for competition. Physical preparation is certainly part of the story. It has been said that performance is 95% physiological and 5% psychological, however what most athletes do not understand is that the 5% psychological, rules the 95% physiological.

Consider this fact; performers follow almost identical training regimens, yet during a competition there is one winner in each event. What separates one athlete from another? In many cases, perhaps even most cases, mental preparation is the deciding factor. To be a good athlete, psychological training is essential, and compared to physical conditioning it is generally easier and more enjoyable.

There is no doubt that athletes need psychological conditioning (mental skills) to attain their optimal performance. Mind and body need to work together. Excess tension, distractions and misdirected focus are negative factors that mental skills can help control and, thus allow athletes to perform at their best. However, if these factors are not controlled and work against the athlete, these psychological factors are so powerful they can easily negate thousands of hours of physical training. The psychological skills necessary to perform well are fairly straightforward: relaxation, concentration, imagery, self-talk and a pre-competition mental routine. It is my observation that the modern-day student athlete brings with them a uniquely different skill set and mindset than in the past, and of course that brings its own set of challenges.

One of my colleagues, who is an amazing educator and has been teaching for over 30 years, echoes the same sentiment stating that "students in increasing number are showing up to the classroom disengaged and distracted which has greatly increased the potential for crisis, significantly reducing the chance of achieving the desired outcomes." Educators are, more now than ever, expected to be responsible for not only academic growth of each individual student as evaluated by state testing, but they are also expected to develop lesson plans that address the multiple intelligences in the classroom, be experts in content areas outside of their wheelhouse, be mediators, a community liaison, a counselor, and often times the primary caretaker for both before and after school care. Parents are often less engaged, unwilling to partner on behavior concerns and teachers are expected to spend not only time, but also extensive financial resources to increase motivation, engagement and entertainment.

I have seen the same things in the athletic arena and *despite what the student/student athlete brings to the table my goal, desire and responsibility is to expect and solicit their very best.* I know that to position my student athletes for the best chance of success, it is imperative that I forge a link between attention and excellence. This can be easier said than done, however when we learn to play by the "5/95 rules of human performance" everyone wins!

The Importance of Focus

The answer to every question is what is the goal? If the goal is to build a better student athlete then I must look beyond a certain level of giftedness, skill or innate ability. I shouldn't put the cart before the horse. In essence, I should begin by teaching them a skill that will help them improve in all areas of their life. If this is the construct from which I will be working, it is apparent that the single most important skill is to focus.

The skills of concentration and focus are probably the most important of all the psychological skills to affect actual performance.

I have always been intrigued and fascinated with individuals, teams and organizations that reach extraordinary levels of success and why others, though highly capable, are not nearly as successful. As a coach I have worked with many who have been on the precipice of greatness, with certain victory in sight yet slipped into mediocrity. The lack of success wasn't because of the lack of some innate skill, a poor work ethic or negative attitude. I believe that one of the major culprits is the inability to focus.

For years athletes have heard coaches repeat the words, "Come on now, focus, keep your head in the game!" I wonder if anyone ever really explained what it means to "focus." We always assume an athlete knows exactly how to focus and more importantly how to turn the focus switch on and off. Track and field, for example, is like very few other sports with its requirement to focus. Competitions in basketball, football, tennis, soccer and most other sports tend to last only a couple of hours. Track meets, on the other hand, may last up to eight hours and sometimes longer depending on the weather. This requires the athlete to go from a broad to a narrow focus multiple times within that period of time. An academic day typically lasts between seven and eight hours. A business professional's day is somewhere between eight and twelve hours, which can be incredibly taxing. During the competition season the track and field athlete may only compete once a week, while the student and the business professional are in a competition every day!

The single most frequent cause of mistakes during a performance is to be in the *wrong attentional state*, thus resulting in inappropriate concentration. We are all at different states of readiness. When athletes learn how to control their attentional states, they make fewer errors and become more confident in their ability to perform. *Students are not taught how to concentrate appropriately so they must find a way to accomplish this task themselves.*

I have been coaching for over 31 years and have attended hundreds of workshops and clinics. I have listened to many speak thoroughly about why concentration is important but not necessarily how to accomplish this task effectively.

In any case there have been monumental gains in focus and concentration in the athletic arena. Here's what we have learned. Concentration, arousal, anxiety and self-confidence are intricately related with each of these variables, greatly influencing the others.

Concentration is not interpreted in the same way by everyone. It is difficult to describe as it is composed of different phases, "basically concentration is the focus of attention." This focus can be directed internally or externally. For example, in Colorado Springs the weather has become increasingly unpredictable, so an athlete may have to focus on the wind direction, their opponent, the crowd, etc. each of these being external factors. On the other hand, the athlete may be concentrating on a cue, a thought, a strategy or past performance; all of which are internal factors.

Athletes who have been properly trained in *Mental Routines* and *Mental Focus* can concentrate on external factors and can also focus on a single object or several things at once. And of course, this gives them a tremendous advantage. Again, I am reminded of Victor Frankl's quote;

"Between stimulus and response there is space. In that space is our power to choose our response. In our response lies our growth and our freedom."

We are living in the information age. According to research the typical American hears or reads more than one hundred thousand words every day. Think about that for a moment, 100,000 words EVERY DAY. We are now exposed to more stimuli in ONE WEEK than our ancient ancestors were exposed to in their entire lifetimes.

Everything we are exposed to is a "nutriment" that needs to be "digested." Those 100,000 words we hear and read every day must be processed and digested. If you're the "typical" American, jamming your consciousness so full of words (and stimulation) all day every day, you probably have a very hard time giving the important things your full attention and have a **misdirected focus.**

Consider the following:
- A learned focus is required for upward mobility in life.
- Education is the gateway for upward mobility.
- To create equitable opportunities in education and other areas of our lives, it is critical that we learn how to focus properly.

The ACE Project: Think Say Do

We are currently working with students at an elementary school in the southeastern part of Colorado Springs, Colorado. This elementary school is near and dear to my heart as it happens to be my alma mater! Going back to my old stomping grounds some 50 years later is quite nostalgic, fulfilling and very satisfying. As in most schools, there is a population of students who face a host of disciplinary and other negative issues.

Achieving Competitive Excellence (ACE) is a Character, Integrity, Leadership and Life Skills Development Program. **Think Say Do** is one of the "systems of success" that is implemented through ACE. **Think Say Do** helps students analyze situations in real-time and make the best decisions in that moment. Using our proven coaching model students are guided through novel decision-making approaches which result in improved behavior, increased attention and better classroom performance.

The **Think Say Do** process helps by developing the student's ability to control the Brain's Executive Functions which are needed to achieve any kind of purposeful activity. The **Think Say Do** process provides a stepwise approach to reach a goal or conquer an objective. The brain relies on three essential processes and the **Think Say Do** process addresses all of them:

Attention. The ability to focus on relevant stimuli and block out what is not relevant.
- **Think Say Do** offers a process that inhibits what is disruptive, irrelevant or destructive.

Inhibition: The ability "not to do" certain actions that could be distracting or destructive.

- **Think Say Do** provides structures, disciplines and practices that teach students to attend to what is <u>*most*</u> important.

Working Memory: The ability to access relevant information for reasoning, decision making and future actions.

- **Think Say Do** helps students become conscious of what they need to make the right decisions.

Think Say Do sessions are instructed (cues) in such a way that enables students to attend, inhibit, and remember.

In other words, we are training our students to be able to:

- Focus on something specific.
- Stay on track by not focusing on or being <u>*assaulted*</u> by other data inputs or toxicity.
- Maintain continuous awareness of relevant information at all times.

The initial results of the ACE Project are extremely promising. On the next few pages you will see a step by step explanation of one of the mental mastery routines we use to help support the **Think Say Do** process.

Mental Mastery Routines

Let's look at a simple mental mastery routine designed to improve focus. Before we dive into the work at hand, we walk the students through a 3-minute mental mastery routine.

Step 1. The students are instructed to close their eyes. In many cases this is not an easy thing for a student to do. Our students come from various backgrounds and have faced many challenges. To achieve the desired outcome, you will have to establish rapport and trust with the student. The action of closing the eyes is very important simply because when the eyes are closed it helps decrease the stimuli and promotes an internal awareness. *It is important to learn to listen to the inner self.* This is not an easy thing to do but with practice it certainly can be done.

Step 2. With their eyes closed we encourage them to turn their attention inward and focus on their breathing or heart rate. For the student to accomplish this task, they must silence their mind. Students are asked to place their hands on their chests and feel the chest rise and fall with every breath.

Step 3. The next step is to pay attention to the internal narrative, attend to their thoughts, asking questions such as; are your thoughts pessimistic or optimistic and are you experiencing rapid brain cycling (RBC), etc. The goal is to develop a *deliberate, intentional intelligence* about what is occurring in their mind, acknowledge what they are experiencing, and ultimately teach them to release any negativity they may be experiencing.

Step 4. The final step is to place themselves with their favorite person, place or thing (noun) and emotionalize it. Students are instructed to make a concerted effort to establish a positive, realistic picture, employing thoughts, feelings and actions!

Here is the simplified version of the three-minute mental mastery model.

1. Close your eyes.
2. Turn your attention inward (focus on breath or heart beat).
3. Attend your thoughts (pessimistic, optimistic, or RBC), acknowledge and release.
4. Place yourself with favorite person, place or thing (noun) and add emotion. *Make a concerted effort to establish a positive, realistic picture employing thoughts, feelings and actions.*

We use a *similar* 3-minute mastery model in the athletic arena. Each practice begins the same way without exception. We call it our mental tune-up! It is a 5-step process instead of the 4-step process used in the classroom. The mental tune-up is followed by a physical routine that will support the operative skill we are working on that day. I am the executive director of SPEED T&F, a national caliber youth athletic educational program. SPEED is the acronym for **S**ystematic **P**rogram to **E**nhance **E**ducational **D**evelopment. SPEED is recognized as one of the best track and field programs in the country. This program carries an amazing GPA of 3.86. While the national average for athletes receiving scholarships to attend college is a dismal a two percent, SPEED's average is an unparalleled eighty-four percent. I share this example with you to demonstrate how this 3-minute mental mastery routine can work in multiple arenas, athletic, academic, corporate etc.

1. Close your eyes.
2. Turn your attention inward (focus on breath or heart beat).
3. Attend your thoughts (pessimistic, optimistic, or RBC) acknowledge and release.
4. Place yourself with favorite person place or thing (noun) and emotionalize it. (Make a concerted effort to establish a positive, realistic picture employing thoughts, feelings and actions.)
5. Select one goal to accomplish.

Developing a mental routine is taking the learned practice or innate ability to concentrate and consciously direct the focus in the right direction. This sort of concentration must be taught, developed and nurtured. <u>The ability to concentrate is not the key. The focus on concentration is the foundation of consistent and confident performance.</u> Excess tension, distractions and misdirected focus can easily negate hundreds of hours of teaching/training. For example, if the goal is for our children is to become excellent students, we must teach them to concentrate and focus. Concentration is the ability to maintain a clear and present focus and focus is the concentration of attention. A good routine is built upon appropriate mental sequencing. Here are a few examples of concentration exercises that when applied regularly yield tremendous results.

Concentration Exercises

1. Narrow External Exercise: Study an object
Take a small object that can easily be held in your hand (ring, coin, earring, paperclip, marble, etc.) and focus intently on the object. If your mind becomes bored and starts to wander (which it will), refocus on the object. Do this for 2-3 minutes; each time you do it change the object.

2. Narrow Internal Exercise: Listen to your own heartbeat
Close your eyes and get into a comfortable position and listen to your heart beat. Try to hear nothing but the heart beating.

3. Broad External Exercise: Awareness exercise
Sit with your eyes closed and just listen to all the sounds that are occurring around you. Do not focus on any one sound, see how many you can detect.

In summary, the benefits of mental routines are as follows:

1. Focus of attention
2. Sustained concentration
3. Control distractions
4. Remove self-doubt or stress producing thoughts
5. Minimize the wandering mind

Focus is a gateway for upward mobility. Excess tension, distractions and misdirected focus are negative factors that will distort what is being heard and how it is being processed. To create an equitable educational or athletic experience for each student, we must build a better student, which begins with teaching them to focus.

Properly implemented mental routines disrupt the systemic cycles of impoverished, faulty thinking and will help create a generation of champions. Through this process we are developing highly disciplined students, with disciplined thoughts, followed by disciplined actions, resulting in improved behaviors, increased attention and better overall performance.

Section Two

Nothing in life, including our circumstances or potential is fixed.
Imagination trumps reality.

Imagery

Imagery is another component of the **Think Say Do** model. Imagery requires us to suspend disbelief. In the previous section I walked you through a stepwise process that helps develop focus. The third step in the process is my favorite. When I instruct students to "place themselves with their favorite person place or thing (noun), making a concerted effort to establish a positive, realistic picture employing thoughts, feelings and actions, they become fully present, thus saying goodbye to yesterday's successes and failures. I am instructing them to suspend disbelief which requires a front side socus.

Imagery is a form of visualization that creates a series of events in the mind. It is a great deal like story telling. We will discuss suspending disbelief further in the pages that follow. For now though, let's warm up our imaginations. As I share the story below I am asking you to become the main character (Allen Eustice) and make a concerted effort to share this experience with him by employing your own thoughts, feelings and actions. Mel Robbins, author of the *5 Second Rule* has performed the research for us and suggests that "spending just 6 minutes per day dreaming and imagining is a way to clean up our thought life."

> Spending just 6 minutes per day dreaming and imagining is a way to clean up our thought life!

There are 5 layers of atmosphere, and in an effort to save time I am choosing to discuss only two, the troposphere and of the stratosphere. The layer closest to the earth is called the troposphere and it extends from sea level to approximately 33,000 feet and it is where weather takes place. As a point of reference, eagles can reach altitudes of 10,000 feet, while the cruising altitude for airplane travel is between 33,000 and 41,000 feet.

The Stratosphere

The stratosphere exists between 33,000 and 166,000 feet. It marks the beginning of what is known as near space. This is the threshold between the planet we experience on the ground and the mysteries of the universe beyond. In order to function in the stratosphere you must wear a pressurized suit (let's pause for a moment so you can put on your imaginary pressurized suit).

Temperatures reach 100 degrees below zero. Air is 1000 times thinner and body fluids begin to boil! I choose to be a stratosphere person rather than the troposphere type. I have developed my very own "_pressurized suit_" that allows me to reach incredible heights and insulates me from some of the challenges faced from the ebb and flow of life.

A Modern Day Iron Man

On Friday, October 24, 2014, Allen Eustice (a former Google executive) and his success entourage set out to do the impossible. It is importatnt to point out that Mr. Eustice needed a team to perform this task. I have learned that when an individual pushes his/her limits they quickly find them. However when a team pushes it's limits, it can MOVE THE EARTH. So this group of dreamers

decided to build a helium balloon that had the capacity to travel from sea level to greater than 130,000 feet. Fully inflated this massive helium balloon would be 525 feet in diameter, roughly the size of a football stadium and at capacity, would require 5000 square feet of helium.

Two years earlier a gentleman named Felix Baumgarter had set the manned balloon flight record by reaching an altitude of 128,907 feet. When I was younger, I wondered why people do the things that they do. Why they push the limits, risking their lives to achieve the impossible. At age 57 I no longer ask why. The answer is simple. It is because they believe they can. For Eustice breaking the record would be a personal challenge, but more important it would be a chance to push the boundaries of human experience. Which begs the question; what is your impossible?

Eustice decided to leave no doubt that he was the ultimate daredevil and chose to push the limits even further. No one had ever attempted to travel into the stratosphere (26 miles into the atmosphere) attached only to a helium balloon and perform the stratosphere jump without a capsule!

What is your impossible?

So well before dawn on Friday, October 24, 2014, near the airport in Roswell, New Mexico, Eustice began his assault on the world record. As Eustice drifted higher whole states appeared and receded. After two hours and seven minutes, Eustice reached his destination of 135,890 feet, which was his float altitude. The helium ballon that had previously looked like an anemic weather balloon, had expanded as far as it could and it would rise so farther. The balloon had performed its job perfectly, was released and drifted off as planned. Eustice, now in a downward position facing earth, started a free fall that would last four minutes and 27 seconds, eclipsing speeds of 822 miles per hour (approximately 365 meters per second). Eustice broke several world records on this day including the world altitude record previously set by Felix Baumgartner. The people waiting on the ground below heard a sonic boom, as Eustice had also traveled faster than the speed of sound.

The exploits of Allen Eustice are mind blowing, moving through the stratosphere at speeds in excess of 822 miles per hour in a pressurized suit, I am reminded of the marvel comics Super Hero, Iron Man. Which, in my opinion, begs some additional questions. If you were a super hero, who would you be? What would your super power be? For me the answers are simple. My super hero is "The Orator" and my super power is expressed through words. Words are singularly the most powerful force to humanity. As I SPEAK I Create (Abracadabra).

Let's Get Physical

So far, I have shared how concentration and imagery are critical to performance. Now let's discuss the significance of a physical routine. At SPEED the mental tune-up is followed by a physical routine specifically designed to improve the bio-motor abilities of speed, strength, coordination, flexibility and endurance. The physiological responses from this routine, composed primarily of neuromuscular integration drills, solicit several different responses from the body both physiologically and psychologically and is crucial to performance e.g., (1) Increase in core temperature (2) Increase in oxygen transport (3) Increase in testosterone levels (4) Stimulate firing pattern, sequencing, monitoring and planning and (5) Force both brain hemispheres to "talk" to each other.

Physical routines set up the biomechanics for the operative athletic skill. However if the physical routine is consistent, and the athlete's mind is wandering, it may be referred to as "going through the motions." The result is a botched or less than par practice. Physical routines without their mental counterparts develop incomplete athletes. It is mental interference which diverts the message sent from the brain to the muscles. The key to successful concentration is to combine both physical and mental routines. STOP THE PRESSES!

The preceding statement infers that mind and body must work together to achieve successful concentration. So what happens when you combine a mental fortitude routine with appropriate physical activity for the purpose of improving classroom performance? Is it possible to improve cognitive performance through physical activity by involving cognitive motor interactions?

The answer is yes! There's a growing body of evidence that has demonstrated the positive cognitive benefits of exercises involving cognitive motor interactions, training on behavioral and neurophysiological measures of spatial working memory in children."

Cognitive Evidence (When the body moves the brain grooves)

Just how important is movement to learning? The vestibular (inner ear) and cerebellar (motor activity) system is the first sensory system to mature. This system is an information-gathering and feedback source for movements. This area is critical to our attentional system, because it regulates incoming sensory data. This interaction helps us keep our balance, turn thoughts into actions, and coordinate movements. That's why there's value in activities that stimulate inner-ear motion, like swinging, rolling, crawling, jumping and cross laterals. Cross laterals use arm and leg crossover activities that can force both brain hemispheres to "talk" to each other better.

Simple Examples of Crossover Activities

- Pat your head and rub your belly is an example of a crossover activity.
- Marching in place while patting opposite knees.
- Patting yourself on the opposite shoulder and touching opposite elbows or heels.

On the next few pages you will find some examples of drills that can be performed in the classroom. We typically perform each drill for approximately 10-15 seconds followed by a 45-60 second recovery. We are currently working to implement these drills into the physical education classes. I think it is awesome when the teachers become "classroom coaches!" When performing these exercises I also suggest having water available for the students!

NI/CMI Drills

This type of neuromuscular integration solicits several different responses from the body both physiologically and psychologically and is crucial to performance e.g., (1) Increase in core temperature (2) Increase in oxygen transport (3) Increase in testosterone levels (4) Stimulate firing pattern, sequencing, monitoring and planning and (5) Force both brain hemispheres to "talk" to each other.

Windmills - General
→ Keeping the shoulders square, place both hands at 12:00
→ Rotate right arm forward into a full circle 360 degrees - drop arm to side
→ Rotate left arm forward into a full circle 360 degrees - drop arm to side
→ Shake it off
→ Rotate right arm backwards into a full circle 360 degrees - drop arm to side
→ Rotate left arm backwards into a full circle 360 degrees - drop arm to side
→ Rotate right arm forward into a full circle 360 degrees - stop at 12:00
→ Rotate left arm backward into a full circle 360 degrees - stop at 12:00
→ Shake it off
→ Right arm full circle 360 degrees - step forward with left leg
→ Left arm full circle 360 degrees - step forward with left leg
→ Shake it off

Windmills - Complex
- → Keeping the shoulders square, place one hand at 12:00 the other at 6:00
- → Rotate right arm forward into a full circle 360 degrees
- → Rotate left arm forward into a full circle 360 degrees
- → Return to 12:00 and 6:00 positions
- → Rotate right arm backwards into a full circle 360 degrees
- → Rotate left arm backwards into a full circle 360 degrees
- → Return to 12:00 and 6:00 positions
- → Rotate right arm forward into a full circle 360 degrees - step out while walking in place
- → Rotate left arm forward into a full circle 360 degrees - step out while walking in place
- → Shake it off and repeat

Crossover Laterals
- → March in place while patting opposite knees
- → March in place while patting self on opposite shoulder
- → March in place while touching opposite elbow
- → March in place while touching opposite heels
- → Pat head while rubbing tummy

Straight Leg Bound
- → Body upright, flex thighs
- → Shuffle in place with knees in a locked position
- → Maintain toe up position
- → Lift heel 4 inches off the ground striking the ground with the ball of the foot

Exercise is Medicine

Most of us understand the benefits of exercise in terms of improving physical conditioning, strength, weight loss, etc. However recent findings have discovered that exercise is one of the most powerful interventions to enhance various aspects of brain function including motor learning, cognition, emotional regulation and attention deficit hyperactivity disorder (ADHD). Individuals with ADHD are easily distracted and struggle to focus their attention. Given the benefits of interval exercises for improving executive functions, students with ADHD and self-regulation challenges may benefit from incorporating exercise breaks into the classroom to help refocus their attention, regulate their classroom behavior and improved their overall academic performance.

Interval Training and Improving Brain Function

A good way to explain the effects of interval training on brain function is the upregulation of growth factors, such as brain derived neurotrophic factor (BDNF).
1. BDNF is critical for the growth, functioning, and survival of brain cells.
2. BDNF increases cell to cell communication.
3. BDNF also promotes growth of new brain cells in the hippocampus.

The two key brain regions impacted by interval exercise that directly support cognition are the hippocampus and frontal cortex.
1. Hippocampus is critical for learning and memory.
2. Frontal cortex governs executive functions related to self-regulation and focusing attention.

Interval exercises improve executive functions in both the lab and academic settings. In the academic setting, high intensity exercise breaks improve selective attention in children and in young adults.

ACE Outcomes

On the following pages you will see the outcomes of the ACE program implemented at an elementary school on the southwest side of Colorado Springs, Colorado in 2014. We used a three-prong approach; mental mastery, neuromuscular integration drills and multiple mind body coaching sessions as reflected on the previous pages.

Program Background: The Achieving Competitive Excellence (ACE) program was designed to equip the elementary school student with the confidence, knowledge, skills and ability to develop their own personal plan for success; setting ambitious, yet achievable goals in the classroom, at home and within the community. This program focused on low-income at promise youth. All participants were either on reduced or free lunch.

Outcomes: Through this mind-body stepwise approach we expected the participant to recognize their self-worth, increase overall productivity and increase self-esteem and pride. In addition we believed that if the neuromuscular exercises/drills were applied routinely participants would improve cognitive function i.e., concentration or attentiveness, concept learning, critical thinking and memory. In the end we found that participants demonstrated improvements in personal mastery (the ability to master their thoughts, behaviors and actions), while recognizing performance barriers, including but not limited to; attitude, negative self-talk, current biases, as well as the current filter in which they viewed the world.

Evaluation Method

Results were measured through teacher surveys, feedback and evaluation forms and classroom indicators.

The program initially began with 52 students ranging from K-5th grade. After the 3rd contact it was determined that the most appropriate grade to implement the instruction was 3rd through 5th. The data below reflects 3rd, 4th and 5th grade students.

Data Analysis: Teachers completed surveys (Teacher Survey – 21st Century Community Learning Centers [21st CCLCs]) after students in the 3rd through 5th grade had completed the program. These surveys were distributed as shown in Table 1.

Table 1.

Distribution of Surveys

Grade	# of Students Taking Survey
3rd	12
4th	8
5th	5

In every grade and category, teachers assessed some students as *needing no improvement.* Assuming the program did not induce a regression in these students' behaviors, the program's effectiveness was only measured on students who had demonstrated room for improvement at the start of the program. The following sparkline charts in Figure 1 show a snapshot of the program's impact in 10 assessed performance areas. Full size versions of charts showing the distribution of charts are shown in Annex A.

Turning in their homework on time.	▪█_▪_
Completing homework to your satisfaction.	▪█_ _ _
Participating in class.	▪█_ _
Volunteering (e.g., for extra credit or more responsibilities).	█▪_█
Attending class regularly.	██▪█▪
Being attentive in class.	▪█▪_
Behaving well in class.	██▪_
Academic performance.	▪█_ _
Coming to school motivated to learn.	▪█_ _ _
Getting along well with other students.	▪█_ _

Figure 1. Sparkline of assessed areas

Findings: The survey results indicate positive changes were observed in all measured areas following exposure to the program. Although this project constituted a small sample size; when compared against the U.S. Department of Education's 21st CCLCs afterschool program, the program demonstrated markedly better results. James-Burdumy, Dynarski, and Deke (2008) reported that teachers reported student behaviors of 1,055 students following an average of 81 days of contact time in the 21st CCLC program. Analysis of this data indicated student performance and desirable behaviors actually decreased after exposure to the 21st CCLC program compared against a control group of 880 elementary school students. In comparing the ACE program to the 21st CCLC, the ACE program produced better results in less time at less cost, as shown in Table 2.

Table 2.

Comparison between ACE and 21st CLCC Afterschool Programs

Program	ACE	21st CCLC
Contact Days	61 hours over five months.	81 days over two years (James-Burdumy et al. (2008)
Cost per student/day	$1.79	$3.98 participant per day (Zhang & Bryd, 2006)
Behavioral Impact	Positive	Negative
Academic Impact	Positive	Negative

References

James-Burdumy, S., Dynarski, M., & Deke, J. (2008).After-school program effects on behavior: Results from the 21st Century Community Learning Centers Program National Evaluation. *Economic Inquiry, 46*(1), 13-18. doi:10.1111/j.1465-7295.2007.00074.x

Zhang, J. J., & Byrd, C. E. (2006). Successful after-school programs: The 21st century community learning centers. *Journal of Physical Education, Recreation & Dance, 77*(8), 3-6,12.

Annex A

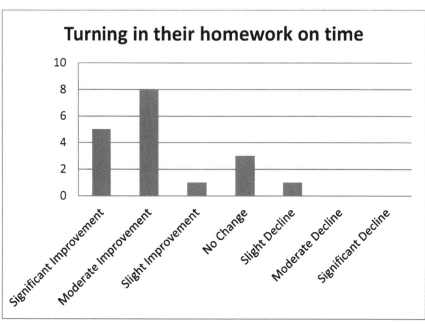

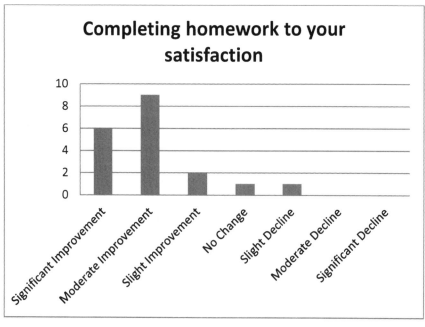

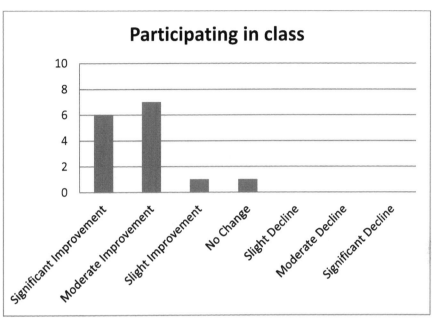

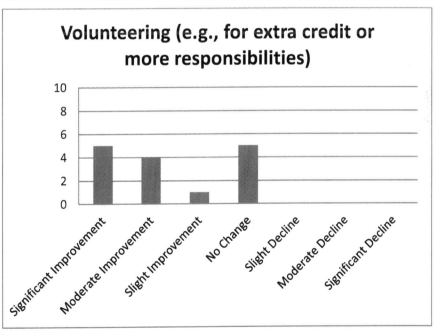

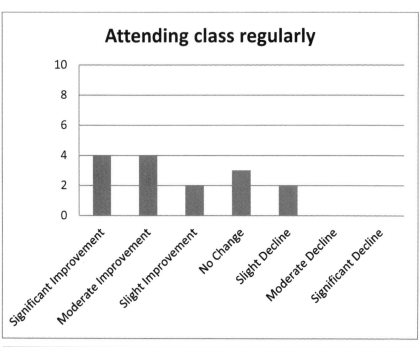

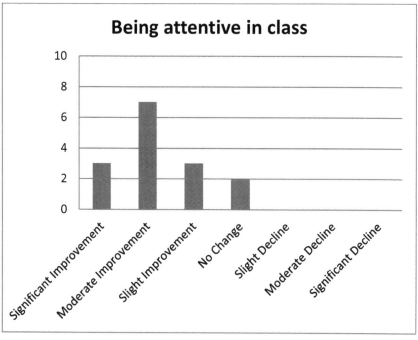

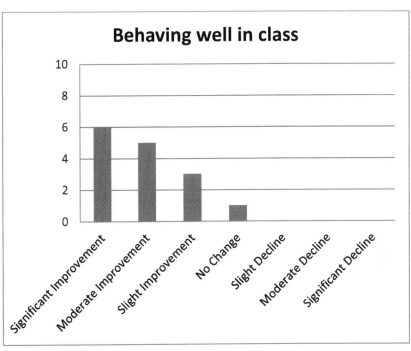

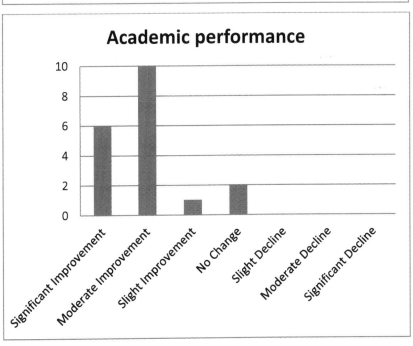

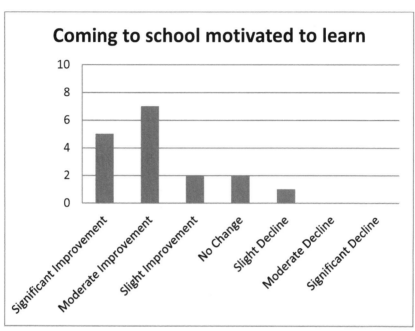

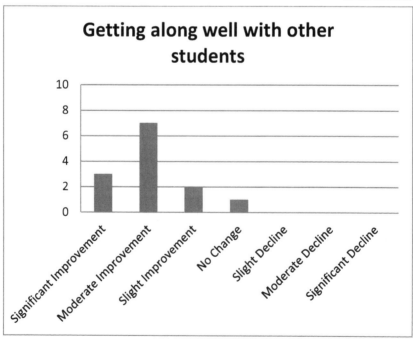

Though this was a small sample size the results were very promising. We now know that properly implemented physical exercise and mental routines improve mental acuity and position students for a greater chance of success!

Section Three

"In the absence of facts, negative thoughts go unchallenged."
Charmas Lee

The Mind is the Battlefield

One thing that I have learned over the last 31 years as a coach is when the athlete has a strong sense of self the opinions of others are less significant. Notice that I said less significant. The opinions of others may still matter, but in the case of negativity, they carry less weight. Additionally, every negative opinion directed at you, responded to positively, creates equity over time! You get stronger every time you don't give in!

> Every negative opinion directed at you, responded to positively, creates equity over time! You get stronger every time you don't give in!

Each day our students are involved in a civil war. It is a war that takes place in their mind. Their mind is the battlefield. At any given moment they are either selling themselves on themselves or selling themselves out. It is important to teach our students how to make good thinking a habit, living each moment in conscious awareness (metacognition).

If we are willing to put in the work and condition our mind for success, we can develop the proper framework for decision making and, over time, develop accurate perceptions, healthy emotions, wholesome desires and honorable intentions.

From the perspective of *emotional intelligence*, utilizing the **Think Say Do** high-performance mental mastery models in a moment of crisis or challenge teaches the student to pause, reflect and not give in to impulsivity, confusion, overwhelming anxiety or a defeatist attitude.

Let's take a look at some of the latest discoveries in neuroscience. According to Dr. Caroline Leif, the author of *Switch on Your Brain,* the following outcomes can be accomplished if we apply the right protocols.

1. We can teach students to use their minds correctly. It is often the hardest step, but it is the first and most powerful step.

2. We can teach the students through conscious effort, to gain control of their thoughts and feelings, and in doing so change the programming and chemistry in their brains.

3. What they are thinking every moment of the day becomes a physical reality in the brain and body effecting their physical and mental health. These thoughts collectively form their attitudes which is their state of mind…and it's their **attitude** not their DNA that determines much of their quality of life.

4. Epigenetics is the physical electromagnetic quantum and chemical flow in the brain that switches groups of genes on or off in a positive or negative direction based on choices or subsequent reactions.

5. Neurogenesis is the birth of new baby cells. This process occurs while we sleep. These new cells are at the disposal of the student to be used in tearing down toxic thoughts and rebuilding healthy thoughts.

I find this information very encouraging. Yes, we can build a better student, friend, spouse, employee, teacher, coach, athlete, etc. but it will require daily efforts of self-improvement.

Learned Helplessness

Martin Seligman was a graduate student at the University of Pennsylvania in the 1960's when he stumbled onto an interesting phenomenon called learned helplessness. It happened when some dogs were given slight electric shocks over which they had no control. No matter what the dogs did, they could not stop the shocks. The shocks simply stopped at random.

Later the dogs where placed in a situation where they could easily stop the shocks. They were put in a box that had a low barrier in the middle of it. All they had to do was to step over the barrier to the other side and the shocks would stop. Ordinarily dogs learn to do this very quickly. They start jumping around and discover that crossing the barrier brings relief. However, the previously shocked dogs learned something different. They *learned* that they were powerless to stop the shocks so, they stopped trying, even though a few steps would have made all the difference. Learned helplessness is the giving up reaction, the quitting response that follows from the belief that whatever you do doesn't matter. Learned Helplessness is real and so is Learned Optimism!

Here is an example of the mindset of a someone who operates from a *learned helplessness* mindset.

"I expect you to <u>let me down</u> and I am going to make sure you do."

Here is an example of the mindset of someone who operates from a *learned optimism* mindset.

"I expect you to <u>make me great</u> and I am going to make sure you do."

I have seen this in the athletic, academic and corporate arena. The good news is that based on the latest discoveries in neuroscience it is possible through conscious effort, to gain control of our thoughts and feelings, and in doing so change the programming and chemistry in our brains. Through repetition, role playing, priming posters and memorization, we can learn a stepwise approach and move away from this systemic faulty thinking! To do this we must first create an environment that is hostile towards mediocrity.

You Can't Average Your Way to Success

Many of you may be familiar with Jim Collins, the author of *Good to Great*. This book sits on the top of my book shelves and has stayed on my captain's list for several years. Mr. Collins shares that to grow a successful company it is important to "create an environment that is hostile towards mediocrity." Hostile towards mediocrity sounds a bit demanding but it makes perfect sense to me. I interpret this to mean that *you cannot average your way to success*. So why don't we establish the same guidelines for our internal infrastructure, our minds?

What if we were to:

- Build an emotionally intelligent structure that will motivate and empower?
- Set limits and boundaries on confusion and distractions?
- Become intolerant to negativity, helplessness, powerlessness or victim hood?
- Develop an environment that is positive, energetic and performance motivated?
- Establish an intentional structure with disciplines and practices that create what we desire?

In order for the brain to organize behavior towards new habits and new ways of performing, it must create new pathways. Our brains, hearts, minds and souls are constructed to perform under certain conditions and dynamics and when these are present, they produce and thrive. *We think, behave, and perform to our capacities.*

We will always get what we create and allow.

It is important to develop the proper psychological and emotional attitude; it will determine how you see life and how others see you. Our mental physiology is one of the greatest predictors of our success and it comes down to three things;

how we THINK
what we SAY
what we DO

A winning attitude is a prerequisite to achieving competitive greatness.

Personal Mastery

Ok it's game time. We are on the road to personal mastery, let's begin by developing the proper *psychological and emotional attitude.* A winning attitude is a precursor to success. Your attitude will not only determine how you see the world, but how others see you. Developing the discipline to develop a winning attitude will not come naturally, easily, automatically, or quickly. Experts suggest that it takes 63 days to create long lasting change. Don't let setbacks or excuses justify quitting, give yourself ample time. You will find that your mind needs time and experience to assimilate these new behaviors.

You cannot manufacture or fabricate change overnight.

To change a behavior, you must first change the **attitude** towards the behavior. Like any new model of behavior this change must be wrestled with, talked through and come to terms with. As time passes, and by the grace of God, you will discover that your change in behavior has positively affected several areas of your life. With this change, you will develop the proper framework for decision making. In addition, you will have given yourself the ability to choose your destination in life.

"Each morning I choose my breakfast, I choose the clothes I wear, I choose my thoughts and I choose my attitude. I choose what I see, say what I see, and seize what I say. I choose my internal narrative, no discussion, no negotiation and no debate. I command my thoughts to become obedient and I choose not to negotiate with failure." Charmas B. Lee

The aforementioned quote reflects a winning attitude and the power of choice. Please read through it again and notice how many times I mention the word choose. Note that I choose the attitude that I will embrace for the day.

This is where we begin to fuse the 5/95 rule of human performance with some of the latest findings in neuroscience.

- Every action is preceded by a thought.
- Thoughts and words are neutral, we assign them value.
- At any moment of the day you are either selling yourself on yourself or selling yourself out. It is imperative that you know what you are thinking.
- Your mind is always eavesdropping on your self talk.

Neurogenesis is the birth of new baby cells. This process occurs while we sleep. These new cells are at our disposal to be used in tearing down toxic thoughts and rebuilding healthy thoughts. When you understand that what you think about expands, you become very careful about what you think about.

Rebuilding healthy thoughts will require the following components;

- Front Side Focus
- PM Ritual
- AM Ritual

Before the professional musician, athlete, celebrity, etc. steps into the spotlight he or she has visualized the performance multiple times. They understand that the body reacts to what it perceives. The psychological system cannot differentiate between real or imagined stimuli. Visualization or what some people refer to as mental rehearsal allows you to simulate a positive performance over and over so that the body is conditioned to react to the real event as it would the imagined event. This must be taught, developed and nurtured. For most of us images of failure tend to occupy our minds because of the fear of failure. I believe that it is possible to make each day a glorified exhibition of brilliance. You've probably seen the posters that say the best way to predict the future is to create it yourself. I agree and believe that it starts in the mind.

We can all use the same system that professionals use to achieve their desired outcomes by developing a front side focus. If your goal is to have an exceptional day on a Monday, then on Sunday night you should implement a PM ritual that will prepare you for the day. Ask yourself the following questions.

The night before... (Sunday Night)
1. What is one thing I can get excited about tomorrow?
2. Word that describes the person I want to be tomorrow.
3. A situation tomorrow that might make me feel anxious, nervous, panic, afraid, sad or angry and how will I positively respond to it.

4. How will I celebrate the successful day?

Creating a front side focus, simply means to plan for what's ahead. By implementing a PM ritual you are giving yourself permission and direction to have a fantastic day. The next step in this process is the AM ritual.

When performing the AM ritual is very important to make the first choice of the day the best choice of the day. We make these teeny tiny decisions all day long and the accumulation of our choices will determine our success or failure.

Enter *Think Say Do*...

As I **THINK** I Become   As I **SPEAK** I Create   I **DO** the Work

Thoughts and word are neutral. I assign a value to them.

Monday Morning

When I wake up Monday morning it's important that I attend to my thoughts and impulses. You would be surprised what goes on in your head, so I choose to silence my mind a bit.

Q. Are my thoughts pessimistic or optimistic?
Q. Do my complaints outnumber my compliments?
Q. Am I holding on to stuff from yesterday?

AM Ritual

Please repeat after me. As I THINK I become.

Once you have checked in and determined what your first three thoughts are, if they are not empowering, uplifting and motivating, select three words that are! My three words are

Powerful-Impactful-Purposeful

These three words reflect the person that I am choosing to be on this day. So I share these three words with my internal self-talk. I must confess to you that when I first began this journey it was not an easy thing to do. Each morning my mind became a battlefield. At any given moment I was selling myself on myself and the next I was selling myself out. I'd lay in the bed and repeat my three words, Powerful-Impactful-Purposeful, over and over and over again. No matter how many times I tried to exchange the negative thoughts for the good ones it just did not work. Day after day, week after week and then finally something happened. I woke up one morning and went through the first step, silenced my mind and checked in and heard my internal narrative whisper...

Powerful-Impactful-Purposeful!

It was unbelievable. According to Napoleon Bonaparte there are "15 minutes in every battle that will determine the outcome of the war". The stronghold that had a grip on my mind was shaken. For weeks my first choice of the day was to attempt to make good thinking a habit. In order to do it I had to live in conscious awareness.

Please repeat after me. As I SPEAK I create.

My thoughts had become 100% congruent with the person I wanted to be, but it wasn't enough to simply think the words, it was time to implement the next step. I would need to SPEAK them into existence. Words are singularly the most powerful force to humanity. As a coach, word selection is critical. Based on how I say what I say, I possess the power to make an athlete's life miserable or joyous. I can humiliate or humor, hurt or heal.

The second step in the AM ritual is to reinforce the three power thoughts with the same three power words. Thoughts and words are neutral, we assign them their value. It is time to deploy the thoughts. First, I must see the three words in my mind's eye. Second, I must say what I see and SEIZE what I say!

There is an inherent power that comes with sound, so when I speak the three words, I speak them powerfully, impactfully and purposefully. It is simple, using my coaching voice I place the words "I AM" in front of them and say;

I AM POWERFUL
I AM IMPACTFUL
I AM PURPOSEFUL

When I apply the words "I AM", I am speaking in the present. I seize what I say! I AM POWERFUL is a statement that inhibits, assaulting toxic thoughts such as I *wish* I was, or I *should* have been, or *could* have been. I AM POWERFUL is about the present, not the past or the future. It is the here and now. There is nothing more powerful than being *dynamically* present! Dynamic presence leads to immediate action which takes me to the third step.

Please repeat after me. I DO with intention, passion and purpose.

It's one thing to think it, another thing to speak it, but you seal the deal when you transfer those thoughts and words into action. Please remember, the likelihood of doing something diminishes the further away you get from the initial moment of inspiration. And your confidence erodes as well. The differentiator between my days that "took flight" versus those that did not was ***immediate action.*** Note my first few actions;

- kiss my wife on the cheek (kissing my wife is an action)
- pat my pup on the head (patting my pup on his head is an action)
- express my gratitude, hydrate, workout (expressing my gratitude is an action)

Here is what I have discovered. Your thoughts and words are ready to take flight and move from *inspirational to operational.* There is a cost for inaction. Choosing not to take action is a prelude to failure.

On the next page you will find a glimpse of the 1st hour of my day.

AM Ritual

1. Think - 3 thoughts or words
2. See - 3 thoughts or words in my mind's eye
3. Say - 3 thoughts or words
4. Seize - 3 thoughts or words (I say what I see & seize what I say)
5. Do with intention, passion and enthusiasm
6. Express Gratitude i.e. wife, dog, feet touch the ground
7. Drink 24-30 ounces of water
8. Affirmation (Set my intention for the day)
9. Don't check my inbox, texts (checks me out of my life)
10. Physical Training - Spiritual Training - Mental Training
11. Fuel
12. Embrace the attitude I will chose for the day!

Embracing the attitude for the day requires one final step, my affirmation.

Affirmations

Reprogramming the subconscious mind to combat negative thinking through the use of powerful words and positive statements.

The final step of the AM ritual is to perform my personal affirmation. I believe that your affirmation should reflect your personality. I am very competitive and possess a strong personality. In this instance it means that I am demanding of myself. Therefore I apply a language that works for me. I also have a vivid imagination. So I like to incorporate words that reflect sights and sounds. Look at my affirmation below.

"I have come to a frightening conclusion.
I am the decisive element in my home, office, church and community.
It is my personal approach that creates the climate.
It is my daily mood that makes the weather.
Because of my mindset I possess tremendous power to make life miserable or joyous.
By choice I am a tool of torture or an instrument of inspiration.
My thoughts and words can humiliate or humor, hurt or heal.
In all situations it is my response that decides whether a crisis will be escalated or de-escalated,
Whether I or others will feel humanized or dehumanized.
With this mindset comes tremendous responsibility and great power.
Today I choose to be a Champion, because when I can champion myself I can give rise to the voice of others."

Now that I have "sealed the deal" I go through my AM Ritual checklist to be sure I haven't missed anything.

AM Ritual Checklist /Scorecard

0 = Poor   1 = Fair   2 = Good   3 = Average

4 = Above Average   5 = Excellent

1. conditioned my mind for success	0	1	2	3	4	5
2. fueled my body properly	0	1	2	3	4	5
3. fueled my spirit properly	0	1	2	3	4	5
4. trust the path God has me on	0	1	2	3	4	5
5. stayed technology free	0	1	2	3	4	5
6. I chose not to consult my emotions	0	1	2	3	4	5
7. set tempo pressed agenda	0	1	2	3	4	5
8. seized attitude for the day	0	1	2	3	4	5
9. set declaration for the day	0	1	2	3	4	5

When I first began the quest to disrupt some of the systemic patterns and thoughts, I had experienced for years it was frustrating and difficult. Several times I reverted back to familiar routines because I didn't see or feel any progress. There was nothing tangible about my efforts. The "chorus of despair" in my head would take over and serve up countless thoughts like, this isn't working, nothing is changing, you are wasting your time, what's the use! I'd spend the first few minutes of the morning verbally sparing with my internal narrative and before you know it this type of mental fatigue would make a coward of me, so I'd raise the white flag of surrender and try again the next day. It turns out that success or failure is typically one thought away.

Each night I journaled my AM experiences. Whenever I chose not to apply the first step of the AM ritual, I didn't follow through with the other steps. I was relatively inconsistent with the first step for the first 16 days. I became more consistent over the next 14 days and for the next 33 days I performed the task and followed through with the completed AM ritual without fail. I estimate that it took 63 days to get into the "habit" of performing the ritual. Basically I fell in love with the process and have been happily married to it ever since!

At some point the behavior became automatic, it freed up tremendous cognitive resources for other things. I didn't have to think about the behavior at all to get it done. It was like brushing my teeth, something I have done every day for 57 years without giving it a second thought. I experienced more energy in the morning and was more creative. In fact it became very uncomfortable when I did not perform my regimen.

Here is what I learned. As much as I knew that it wouldn't be the case, I wanted my progress to be linear, I hoped it would come quickly and it didn't. That is not how things work.

A single decision is easy to dismiss.

The breakthrough hadn't happened because I wasn't consistently persistent. In my mind I was all in, totally committed, however my journal indicated differently. A 100% commitment 39% of the time is only a 39% commitment! I was *consistently inconsistent.* During the first 30 days or so I was experiencing what James Clear discusses in his book, *Atomic Habits,* the "valley of disappointment." The valley of disappointment is defined as *feelings of being discouraged after putting in weeks or months of hard work without experiencing any results.* Basically what you think should happen and what actually happens.

In the world of human performance we understand that it takes approximately 500 hours of visualization to master a complex motor skill like hurdling or triple jumping. These events are so technical that not only is it important to train them physically, but you also must train them visually as well. On average, it takes a novice sprinter approximately 300 properly performed repetitions at the appropriate speed to achieve the nervous system improvement. This will come primarily through drills, skill development, form running and studying video. If the system is corrupted it can take up to 5000 repetitions to re-educate the motor. The higher performing the nervous system, the higher performing the athlete.

Think about this. There is a trade off in running. Every step is a compromise, sacrificing a loss of a horizontal velocity to maintain a dynamic stability. Every joint, tendon and ligament has a certain capacity for power and speed. It is very complex. When we correct an athlete's running mechanics, jump or hurdle technique, there is a period of time that they will tend to run slower. It is very difficult to teach an athlete to be patient and trust their training system when they don't see the improvements in the first few weeks. Frustration, doubt, fear and apprehension kick in. They too find themselves in the valley of disappointment. But with the right mindset, self-efficacy (belief that the training will yield dividends) and consistency of effort the improvements come.

Here is my point. Anything worthwhile requires commitment. There is a good chance there will be a few setbacks, but ultimately success will occur. Athletes have coaches, but the coach doesn't run the race for them. As a coach I've learned that you cannot coach effort. Only through effort, which requires multiple repetitions, will success be found. Here is the good news, at some point the athlete learns how to analyze movements in real time and make critical adjustments in micro seconds. They learn how to stand outside of themselves… and so will you.

Self-Coaching

Let's take a look at what occurs to improve an athlete's performance and how to use this same model to coach ourselves.

- We video the athlete performing the event.
- The coach and athlete view the footage in real speed, then in slow motion.
- A discussion ensues that informs the athlete on what they did well and why.
- There is also a discussion on any errors and how to correct them
- We will only address one correction at a time.
- With the correction in place we film the athlete and start the process over again.
- Sometimes a single correction, corrects all others.

- I journal the events that took place in the day, beginning with my AM routine.
- I take the time to read through them thoroughly.
- I determine what I did well.
- I determine what I didn't do well and why.
- I distill it down to one change to focus on
- I write it down in my PM ritual and visualize the outcome.
- I get a good night's sleep and implement that "one correction" in the morning.
- Sometimes a single correction, corrects all others.

"It's not an issue if it's not an option."

Bright Lines

Bright Lines

Respect the speaker is a bright line. It is a precursor to the **Think Say Do** process. Early in my coaching career I found out that the more rules I had for the athlete, the more time I would spend enforcing them. I learned that if you wanted remarkable results you should simplify, simplify, simplify, so I distilled it down to just one rule, "Respect the Speaker." This one rule, that quickly must become a habit, is what is referred to as a "Bright Line." Bright lines are clear, simple unambiguous boundaries that you do not cross. Bright lines provide a really clear perspective on what is and what is not acceptable behavior. My reason for being intolerant to anyone breaking this rule is simple, "a rising tide lifts all boats-one rule lifts all others." It's the only rule I have and it makes a significant difference.

The by-product of my one and only rule is this:

- students attend to the speaker
- pay attention
- prioritize listening ⟶ asking information seeking questions
- removes unnecessary distractions
- increases focus, attention, etc. (time on task)
- follow through with instruction

Here is a fantastic example of a bright line that I like to share with parents and athletes at the start of each season. The excerpt is titled *I Do Have Favorites*. It was part of an article titled *Training Soccer Champions* by Dorrance and Nash and published in *Track Coach Periodical*.

I Do Have Favorites

"Someone might accuse me of "having favorites" on our team. The implication is that this is a terrible sin. When I was a younger coach, I use to think this was terrible also. You're right. I do have favorites. My favorites are those athletes who most fervently do what I ask of them and take constructive criticism well without debate. To those that do, I give more attention. I talk to them more. I spend more time teaching them. I also expect more of them. The implication is made that my favorites improve more than others because they are my favorites and that is somehow unfair. *Don't mistake cause for effect.*

The fact is that the athletes who come to me ready to learn, ready to listen, ready to act on what they learn, and try it my way even if it is more challenging and difficult than they imagined, are ready to get more out of our program. And they are my favorites. As a coach, I have only one thing to offer an athlete. What I can offer is my attention. This means that I attend to their needs. The reward for good behavior should be attention – attending to their needs. The consequence of inattention, lack of effort, unwillingness or unreadiness to learn, or just plain offensive or disruptive behavior, is my inattention to that athlete. How can it be any other way? If you have three children, and you spend all of your time and energy working with one that displays negative behavior, what does that tell your other two children? It tells them that to capture your attention, they should behave poorly. *What we reward is what we get.*

As a coach, I want athletes who are eager to learn, eager to experiment, to improve, and eager to work hard. I want athletes who come to me for help in developing their mental and physical skills and are willing to accept what I have to offer. Otherwise, why have they come to me? I am going to reward that athlete with my attention. In doing so, I encourage others to become like the athlete above. If I spent my time with the unwilling, and/or disruptive player, the uncaring player, I would only be encouraging undesirable behavior. I want to forge a link between attention and excellence. Excellence is the sense of achieving all that is possible and desired. My way of making this happen is to provide my knowledge and attention to those who "attend" to me. This does result in increased performance for those that do so. I am a good coach, and when I pay attention to a person, that person is going to improve. Over time, this makes it appear that my "favorites" are the better athletes. Not so at all. The better athletes are those that pay attention, and thus become my favorites. What the accusing person doesn't realize is that you must have favorites if anyone is to develop in a positive fashion. The coach's job is to reward those who exhibit positive developmental behaviors. Those are my "favorites", and they should be."

There are a few points that I don't agree with completely in the article, however I am sure you get my point when it comes to bright lines.

"Every man's work, whether it be music or pictures or literature or architecture or anything else, is always a portrait of himself."

Samuel Butler

Sense of Self

In psychology, the sense of self is defined as the way a person thinks about and views his or her traits, beliefs, and purpose within the world. It is a truly dynamic and complicated concept because it covers the inner and outer self. Our self-concepts are often cultivated and nurtured in our homes, schools, playgrounds, through our families, friends and teachers. Identities are often imposed or at least encouraged by environmental or cultural forces. For example, if a child is routinely told, "You are really smart" the likelihood is increased that intelligence will figure prominently in the child's sense of identity. In contrast, when a child routinely hears, "You can't do anything right", then incompetence is likely to be central to his sense of self. It can be the same way in a marriage. If one spouse tends to belittle the other or uses a "dark sarcasm" the accumulation of the negative comments can create a toxic environment that promotes a poor sense of self. On the other hand when words are spoken that are uplifting there is a good chance that the spouse sees themselves in a positive light.

Amid a flood of techniques for self-fulfillment many are crippled by confusion, have thrown away their confidence and lack self-esteem and pride. There is an epidemic of obesity, depression, suicide, personal emptiness and escapism through the use of consumerism, drugs and alcohol. We live in echo chambers, the things around us shape our thoughts and can easily make us satisfied or dissatisfied with our present condition.

There is a quote by Thomas Cooley that speaks volumes about the power of outside influences.

"I am not who you think I am
I am not who I think I am
I am who I think you think I am."

I encourage you, not to throw away your confidence. *The stronger the sense of self, the less we concern ourselves with the opinions of others.* To grow your confidence it is important to get acquainted with your best self, lesser self and develop a blueprint to connect your current self with your future self. It is important to develop a vision, simply because excellence is inspired by vision. It is equally important to establish a mission, because your mission gives you permission to be bold and courageous. When an individual begins to experience obstacles, road blocks or physical or emotional pain in the heat of battle, the brain, whose primary role is self-preservation, asks the question, "Why must I suffer?" The individual with a clear mission will answer the question with the vision they have carefully constructed and will continue to fight. Many people have not developed a mission and do not possess a vision, so they quit as soon as they hit a bump in the road or when the pain kicks in.

Let's begin the process of creating a blueprint to improve performance and achievement by completing the exercises on the next 2 pages.

Strengthening the connection between our current self and our future self is vital to our success both personal and corporate.

3 Words that describe my BEST self

_____

_____

_____

Conditions that promote BEST self

_____

_____

_____

3 Words that describe my LESSER self

_____

_____

_____

Conditions that promote LESSER self

_____

_____

_____

3 Words that describe my FUTURE self

_____

_____

_____

Efforts that describe active pursuits

_____

_____

_____

Once you have determined the attribute and conditions that reflect the BEST you, it is important to ask yourself the questions below on a daily basis.

Connect your future self with your current self.

1. Do your current behaviors reflect the person you want to be?

    Yes or No

2. Is your current ritual helping your reach your goal?

    Yes or No

3. Does your current attitude reflect the person you want to be?

    Yes or No

4. Are your current habits supportive of you being the BEST you?

    Yes or No

5. Does your current work effort reflect the person you want to be?

    Yes or No

6. Would those in your inner circle respond the same way you have?

    Yes or No

Vision

Florence Chadwick was the first woman to swim the English Channel in both directions. This was an amazing accomplishment. Driven by ambition she also wanted to be the first woman to swim the 21 miles from the Catalina Islands to the California shore. After months of training she attempted to achieve what many deemed impossible for a woman. The day was July 4, 1952. On this 4th of July morning the water was bone chillingly cold and the fog was very thick, so thick she could not see the shore line. Nonetheless she made her way into the water and began the quest to cover the 21 miles.

Several times sharks had to be driven away with sticks to protect her. She swam for 15 hours and ultimately determined that she couldn't go on. Folks that were alongside her in the boats encouraged her to keep swimming indicating that she was very, very close to her destination. All she could see was dense fog. Unable to see the shoreline she became disheartened and was pulled into the boat.

It was later revealed to Chadwick that she was only 800 meters from the shore when she conceded. In her interview Chadwick indicated that she had been defeated not by fatigue or even the cold, the challenge was that she could not see the shore line. Two months later she swam the same channel and beat the men's record by 2 hours.

Florence Chadwick's story is a great example of the power and importance of vision. I like to keep things simple. I begin with the end in mind and ask myself this question. What will my life look like victorious? I pick three or four categories that are important to me. This provides clarity and a great starting point.

1. Personal

_____

_____

2. Family

_____

_____

3. Academic

_____

_____

4. Professional

_____

_____

5. Community

_____

_____

"Mastering the physics, politics and psychology of *conflict* (fear, anger), are vital to success, both personal and corporate."

Sun Tzu

Mindset

Sun Tzu was made the general of the kingdom of WU sometime between 100-300 B.C.E. Under his leadership, Wu's armies were virtually invincible. In the two thousand years that followed, his military genius served as an example of power and victory to both civilian and military leaders. Sun Tzu believed that mastering the physics, politics and psychology of *conflict* were vital to success, both personal and corporate. This approach to competition and strategy, when used for personal mastery makes his insights as relevant to today's competitive need for self-knowledge as they were to warfare in Ancient China.

Enmity is defined as a deep and bitter hatred, usually shared between enemies. However when we live a life that is 100% incongruent to who we want to be we are at enmity with ourselves. Conflict is a part of life. It is important that we develop tools and a comprehensive strategy to deal with it. The strategy that I am going to introduce you to is the one we instruct our elementary and middle school students to use. It is not just for these students. It will work for whoever applies and practices the strategy. Ultimately it comes down to emotional regulation. Sometimes it very difficult to regulate emotions. It takes practice, practice, practice.

Fixed Mindset

My friend and mentor, Hector Romanos, says that "failure is no match for perseverance." Those who see failure as evidence that they lack the necessary ability or skill will give up and quite logically in light of their belief, never achieve what may have been possible. *If you fight for your limitation's you get to keep them.*

Growth Mindset

If you believe that failure is a part of the success formula, and follow each step as properly designed despite setbacks, your *response-ability* will get dramatically better and eventually you will be able to analyze these situations in real time. In a sense you will gain the ability to *stand outside of yourself* much like the skill the hurdler possesses when they make adjustments on the fly!

Having an emotional outburst, pushing or punching a wall or another student, instead of thinking the behavior through, may appear to be more gratifying in the moment. However you will find that mastering conflict is really more empowering.

Following is the 4-step process to move towards becoming a CHAMPION.

Step 1. De-escalate
De-escalation in this case means to walk away. Walking away decreases the impulse to say or do anything. When the adrenaline is high, cortisol levels rise. Cortisol is the main hormone involved in stress and the flight or fight response. High levels of cortisol impair cognitive performance. Walking away will allow the mind to begin to clear.

Step 2. Diffuse
While walking away perform the calming breath exercise and inhale to a mental count of 4. Hold this breath at the top of the inhalation for a mental count of 4. Exhale s-l-o-w-l-y to a mental count of 8. Hold again for a mental count of 4 before beginning again. After a few cycles of this type of breathing ideally your body

is more relaxed and your mind is clearer. It takes time and practice to breathe this way.

Step 3. De-construct
Now that the body is more relaxed and the mind is clear you can organize your thoughts, virtually creating a story board of the events in your mind. This process is critical to helping you establish your next step and if necessary, explain to someone in authority what occurred.

Step 4. Decide
You have gone through the previous 3 steps and now you have the power to decide what you will do next. At the bottom of the 30 second drill exercise (next page) are three statements that will come into play at this point.

I choose the behavior
I choose the consequence
I choose to be a CHAMPION!

There is nothing more empowering than being in the driver's seat.

30 second drill

I have 30 seconds to choose my response.

How I feel about something

and how I respond to it is up to me.

Step 1. De-escalate ⟶ walk away

Step 2. Diffuse ⟶ calming breath exercise

Step 3. Deconstruct ⟶ organize thoughts

Step 4. Decide ⟶ choose wisely

I choose the behavior

I choose the consequence

I choose to be a CHAMPION!

"True discovery consists not in seeking new landscapes but seeing old landscapes with new eyes."

Marcel Proust

You Find What You Are Looking For

In the early stages of performing the ***Think Say Do*** AM ritual a poster with the three power words selected i.e., POWERFUL-IMPACTFUL-PURPOSEFUL, is placed in a location that can be seen immediately upon awakening. It was very important for me to see them so they would form an imprint in my mind. Basically I could see the words in my mind's eye and no longer had to see them physically. You find what you are looking for. We train our eyes to see what we want them to see. Here is an example.

I really enjoy donuts. There, I said it! Especially the gourmet type. About 6 months ago I went to a place called HURTS DONUTS. The place is amazing. They never close. They claim to be open 25 hours a day and 8 days a week. They have an ambulance parked up front that is decked out with donut attire and provides a delivery service. My favorite donut is the maple bacon bar. Carbohydrates, maple frosting and lots and lots of bacon. I reward myself with the maple bacon delight about once every two weeks! Over a 6-month period I visited the establishment 12 times. They have some pretty cool pictures on the walls. There was one that captured my attention every time I visited the location. It was a pair of fists with the letters HURTS DONUT written on the knuckles. The 10ᵗʰ time I stopped in my wife Janice asked me this question, "every time you come here you spend a big chunk of time looking at that picture. What are you looking for?" I responded, "nothing really, it's just a cool picture." She said, "you are drawn to the picture because there is something unique about it, but you don't know what it is." Janice laughed and said, "the image has 6 digits. Five fingers and a thumb on each hand." She was right!

Remember Marcel Proust's quote "true discovery consists not in seeking new landscapes but seeing old landscapes with new eyes?" Seeing old landscapes through new eyes requires daily practice. *You learn to dig a little deeper, look a little further.* You learn to look for the unseen.

You cannot see the words you speak, but words have tremendous power. I have learned there is power in saying what you see, but only if you follow up by seizing what you say. Once I had trained myself to see the three words, POWERFUL-IMPACTFUL-PURPOSEFUL, in my mind's eye, I'd speak them BOLDLY without any ambiguity. It's one thing to declare something, another thing to take hold of it. If you say it, mean it. If not, it creates cognitive dissonance. There is an inherent force that comes with sound.

I Say what I See and I Seize what I Say!

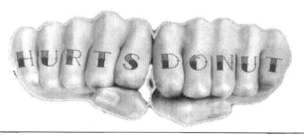

In an effort to remind our students to practice the ***Think Say Do*** principles we created posters for them that lines the hallways. These posters are also strategically posted near the classroom doors directly in the line of sight for the student entering the classroom.

"I Say what I See

and I Seize what I

Say"

As I **THINK** I Become

As I **SPEAK** I Create

I **DO** the Work

This previous poster serves several purposes.

1. Primer - Prompt

The student has a constant reminder of the ***Think Say Do*** philosophy. Not only do they see it physically, they begin to see it in their minds eye. It helps them attend to their thoughts.

2. Anchor Statement - Cue

I Say what I See and I Seize what I Say reminds them of the power of their thoughts and words and puts them in the proper state of readiness.

3. Behavior Trigger

The student knows they are on audition. They take a moment to stand outside of themselves and ask the question, "Do my current behaviors reflect the person I choose to be?"

To determine if a student is checked in, I will often begin a session by reciting the first three words of the ***Think Say Do*** mantra. It is always nice when the students can finish the sentence. Speaking in my coaching voice I say "As I think, and hopefully they'll say, I become. Either way it provides me with an opportunity to ask the following questions.

Q. What does The ***Think Say Do*** poster remind you to do?
Q. When should you apply the 30 second drill?

By asking these questions we position the student for a greater chance of success.

Performance Enhancing Thoughts

"Our actions can be no wiser than our thoughts. Our thinking no greater than our understanding."

George S. Clason

Whatever you agree with will fill your heart, mind and thoughts, and is what you will release into the world around you. If you are willing to change your thinking you can change your outcomes. A couple of years ago we introduced our system of success (**Think Say Do** and Bright Lines) to a group of college students. The name of the program was True Grit. The purpose of the program was to motivate, educate and inspire the students to develop a sense of greater expectations within themselves. We hoped this approach would develop grit and resiliency, ultimately helping decrease the natural attrition that occurs in this realm.

The topics of discussion were designed to help students view ideas with new clarity, refine and shape them into brilliant insights which would result in new opportunities. Using performance enhancing thoughts, we strove for consistency, bringing their thoughts into alignment with their words, and their words into alignment with their actions. Whether the goal was to develop a positive work ethic and attitude, achieve good grades, increase self-confidence, etc. it started with improving their thought life and of course for many it changed their whole life.

In 2017 we executed the True Grit program at a community college in Colorado Springs, Colorado. Over the course of an academic quarter, we interacted with 298 students. At the end of the nine-week program with 112 contact hours, we gave students the opportunity to provide feedback by asking them, "How effective was the True Grit program in influencing your behaviors?" The results of the Likert-scaled responses, e.g. *very much*, *moderately*, *slightly*, and *unknown*, are shown in Figure 1 with *effectiveness* represented by the aggregation of the two highest responses.

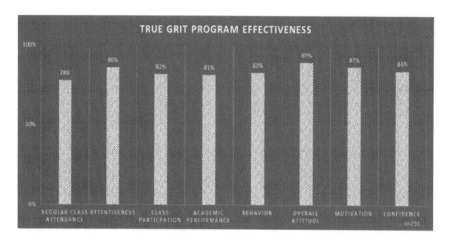

Figure 1. 2017 True Grit Program Performance.
Adapted from 2017 End of Course Survey of the True
Grit Program by J. L. Huisingh, 2017, Clovis Point
Research: Colorado Springs, Colorado.

This average effectiveness rate across the eight measures shown was 84%. These attitudes were corroborated using a coded-thematic analysis of 331 free form qualitative responses from 288 students to the question, "Please describe how the True Grit program impacted your life, either in or out of the classroom." 95.5% of the responses were positive with the results shown in Figure 2.

TRUE GRIT RESPONSE THEMES

n=331 responses from 288 students

Figure 2 True Grit response themes based on open-ended questions regarding program influenced outcomes. Adapted from 2017 End of Course Survey of the True Grit Program by J. L. Huisingh, 2017, Clovis Point Research: Colorado Springs, Colorado

Motivation emerged as the most prolific theme and applied to students' views of life both in and out of the classroom. 27% of comments concerned attitudinal change largely focused around motivation and inspiration. Some examples follow:

- *Before I had no motivation but now, I strive to succeed and fight for the things I want.*

- *True Grit helped me both in and out of the classroom. It was very effective in motivating me and showing me the value of my worth.*
- *I come to class more often and have a positive attitude towards everything.*
- *I already did really well in school, but it really helped with my attitude and confidence outside of class.*

Responses concerning *actions and outcomes* comprised 22% of the comments and indicated program participants both contemplated the impact of their actions as well as implemented changes in their lives with positive results.

- *Well I quit smoking, so I think that is great.*
- *I woke up one day and the think-say-do got me out of bed when I did not want to.*
- *It made me decide to take chances, and now I have a job because I took the chance to ask.*

Participants reported (14% of comments) a change in their *outlook on life*, to include fundamental self-image adjustments.
- *It taught me how to put myself first.*
- *The program helped me maintain and improve my self-worth.*
- *The True Grit program has really helped me to check any negative behavior that I may have had. I'm more aware of how to maintain a positive attitude towards my life.*

True Grit participants reported *confidence* improvements (14% of comments). Several students linked confidence with a reduction in risk aversion.

- *Gave me the confidence to get through my classes and not to give up on them.*
- *It made me decide to take chances.*
- *Before meeting Coach Lee my confidence level was very low. Every day I work on my confidence and have come a long way since the first class.*

Lastly, students provided comments on goals. These comments were often related to the confidence to achieve them.

- *Influenced me to complete my dream of starting my own business.*
- *Instead of being confused with my path this allowed me to slow down, see what I want in life, and how to get there.*
- *Help(ed) me realize my goals and procrastinate less.*

The survey revealed that students improved their level of self-awareness, set goals, and were motivated to action with elevated risk acceptance and a reduction in fear. Students reported the True Grit program proved beneficial both in an out of the classroom with one participant reporting the program influenced potentially life-extending behavior (smoking cessation).

The survey also showed a high-level of participant support for the True Grit program. While some students expressed initial skepticism at being required to take the program, almost all students found value in it. Of the 4.5% of students who did not think the program led to self-improvement, not one participant commented negatively on the program.

Building Champions: Think Say Do In Action

I am a big fan of legendary football coach Vince Lombardi. He took over a downtrodden Green Bay Packers team in 1959 and turned it into professional football's most dominant organization of the 1960s. Lombardi, a tireless worker with exacting standards, led Green Bay to five championships in nine seasons as head coach. His Packers won the first two Super Bowls, and the trophy given to the league champion now bears his name. I believe he is the greatest professional football coach in history. Coach Lombardi has many quotes, however my favorite is *"Gentlemen we are going to relentlessly pursue perfection, knowing full well we won't catch it. Because nothing is perfect. But we are going too relentlessly CHASE – IT, because in the process we will catch excellence. I am not remotely interested on being just good."* Vince Lombardi inherited a team that would be considered capable, but unsuccessful, or "high flyers low achievers." In the end they became champions.

As a coach of over 31 years I have developed a keen insight as to what it takes to develop a champion both on and off the field. A team is composed of a group of individuals. It is often the quality and characteristics of the leader that can inspire an individual to reach beyond their true potential. I recently had the opportunity to work with a group of young boys who fit the category of "high flyer low achiever." These students were certainly capable of doing better but in terms of behavior and academic performance they were missing the mark. During my first encounter I worked on developing rapport and expressed my belief in their ability to achieve success in various areas of their lives. I was honest about the *deliberate* work that would be required, but also painted a picture of what the sweet fragrance of success *could* be like for them.

I implemented the undulating periodization model which I have used in the past to train world class performers. This model is easily adoptable to the academic and corporate environments. It begins with deliberate practice which requires deliberate effort. We met strategically (using the undulating periodization model) eight times over a twelve-week period. The duration of each meeting was forty-three minutes and the location was the library. One specific topic was introduced with a simple assignment to perform before I'd see them again. If applied, it would help them achieve the best chance of success. The assignment required them to "work on their craft 15 minutes a day." Initially students would invent ways to disrupt the session.

Once, while dealing with a disruptive student, I posed this question. "Can I have your permission to share with you and the class how you are *failing yourself?*" His response was typical. "I don't care what you do" he responded. "Thank you, my friend" I said, and I briefly shared with absolute clarity, the three things that he was doing that *guaranteed his success as a failure*. I finished my communication with the following comments; "Young man, I am responsible to you, not for you. I take no responsibility in your success or your failures, I simply give you the tools."

There are several types of coaching styles. The style of coaching used to address the young man in the above paragraph is considered to be authoritative. I have found in parenting and coaching that the authoritative style of coaching seems to work best. According to Madeline Levine, Ph.D. and author of the *Price of Privilege* "authoritative parenting is warm and accepting but at the same time clearly defined limits and expectations are set and expected."

While I believe that you cannot coach effort, I do believe that you can coach excellence. The comments that follow are from a school administrator regarding his thoughts and evidence-based outcomes of this approach.

1/29/19

Charmas worked as a structured mentor/teacher for a cohort of African American males at our school. During this time Charmas focused on essential adaptive skills essential to academic and social success in and out of the school setting. His skills are extraordinary and success evident (e.g.) the growth of the CMAS assessment of the African American cohort at our school surpassed all other sub groups including the Gifted and Talented population. The process Charmas utilizes can be summarized in two words: grit and resiliency. His programming homes in on building essentials skills; a process through which students develop a cognitive strategic plan that breaks larger issues into smaller more manageable ones. The focus on grit/resilience affords his students the opportunity to internalize both problem solving skills and cognitive flexibility-skills essential to overcoming impediments and success in the 2st century.

Interestingly enough several of these young men were part of the school's 8th grade basketball team. As they worked on their individual outcomes, both academically and personally, through the **Think Say Do** coaching, they also went on to win their first ever city basketball championship as a team.

Before we go any further, I should share that *although* I am a human performance specialist, my connection to education runs the spectrum from elementary through collegiate environments. I started working in academia in the early 1990's at the Colorado School for the Deaf and Blind as a Special Education Technician and am currently in Colorado Springs implementing the Achieving Competitive Excellence (ACE) program into select primary and secondary schools. I have worked with 2- and 4-year college institutions in an effort to decrease attrition and provide a blueprint for performance and student achievement. Along the way I have met some amazing educators, none more impressive than Patricia Dennard. Patty has been kind enough to share her thoughts and write a segment titled, **Think Say Do** from an Educator's Perspective.

Patricia Dennard is the owner of Thrive, PLCC. She has been involved in education for over 24 years, serving and supporting students, staff and parents in many roles. Patricia has been an educational assistant, teacher, counselor, behavior interventionist and administrator. Patricia has worked in residential care settings, in 4 different school districts and provides services as a clinician in her private practice as a Nationally Certified (NCC) Licensed Professional Counselor (LPC) Registered Play Therapist (RPT)and Certified Clinical Trauma Professional (CCTP).

Think Say Do from an Educator's Perspective
By: Patricia Dennard MA, LPC, NCC, RPT, CCTP

"Recovery needed!" is heard screeching over the walkie talkie, BANG! CRASH! HUMPH! A chair crashes into a desk, a door slams and a student is heard cussing and threatening others as that student runs out of the classroom and down the hall where a kindergarten student is knocked over by the enraged child pushing through a class line. Crying screams pierce the ears of peers close by as that child is taken to the office to be seen by the nurse.

This is just one of many moments in a school day regularly experienced by school staff across the nation. At any given moment, both students and staff are in need of immediate assistance for not only academic difficulties, but also for social emotional support and encouragement. Although I am not a parent, I have been an educator for the last 24 years, and I can only imagine the number of opportunities parents, guardians and caregivers have every day to redirect, reinforce and instruct their children in hopes of supporting and molding a successful, productive and self-sufficient community citizen.

It is evident, that it truly takes a village to raise a child and that every player in a child's life has a significant impact. I genuinely mean EVERYONE! The impact is variable and can be either positive or negative, but none-the-less, we must remember that WHAT WE DO MATTERS! It is like the ripple affect seen and felt as a pebble is tossed into water. The ripples reach far and wide across many people and environments.

In the book, Help For Billy, Heather Forbes eloquently describes how we must approach problems or ways to reinforce the things we want to continue. She states that if we, "...see every problem as a "nail," ... and the only tool we have is a hammer, we must add tools to the toolbox." (p.1). This is why, after going through three Master's programs and receiving my clinical license, it was evident that I still did not have all the right *tools* for the jobs I was faced with every day. It is not only children who need a tool chest filled with hundreds of ideas and methods of problem solving, but I have found adults are just as in need. I know, because I am one of them! No, seriously, life is a path of progress. It is a process that is ever growing and changing to meet the demands set in front of us every day. I have found that learning about trauma and the effects of trauma are essential elements to addressing challenges we face, young and old alike. I have extensively studied trauma informed care and have become a Certified Clinical Trauma Professional (CCTP) because of the difference it makes when one understands how trauma can affect a child's development and academic success. Trauma informed practices can greatly influence both academic and social emotional outcomes.

In schools today, school staff are trained in best approaches to address the educational and social emotional needs of children, but as I mentioned, it takes a village. Although it is thought that caregivers know their children the best, but even they can benefit from personal support and guidance in caring for their own needs and secondly the needs of children and others. This is just like what is necessary to do on an airplane when faced with the pressure in the cabin changing and the face masks dropping with oxygen. We must tend to the needs of ourselves before we can benefit others. These concepts are not new, but often get forgotten in the busy, task-oriented society in which we live. Maslow's Hierarchy of needs is commonly referred to in terms of meeting basic needs first. In a 2017 online publication for Psychology Today, the author Neel Burton, M.D. who is a psychiatrist, philosopher and writer clearly references and defines the hierarchy.

"In his influential paper of 1943, *A Theory of Human Motivation*, the American psychologist Abraham Maslow proposed that healthy human beings have a certain number of needs, and that these needs are arranged in a hierarchy, with some needs (such as physiological and safety needs) being more primitive or basic than others (such as social and ego needs). Maslow's so-called 'hierarchy of needs' is often presented as a five-level pyramid, with higher needs coming into focus only once lower, more basic needs are met." (Burton, 2017).

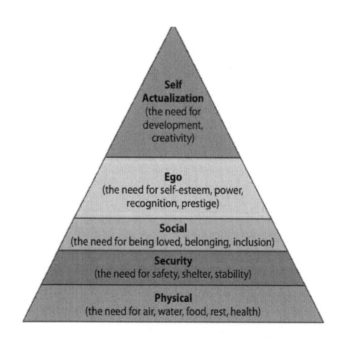

Self Actualization
(the need for development, creativity)

Ego
(the need for self-esteem, power, recognition, prestige)

Social
(the need for being loved, belonging, inclusion)

Security
(the need for safety, shelter, stability)

Physical
(the need for air, water, food, rest, health)

Maslow's Hierarchy is further clarified by Simply Psychology in 2018 and in the 3rd edition of Maslow's book called *Motivation and Personality.*

1. **Physiological needs** - these are biological requirements for human survival, e.g. air, food, drink, shelter, clothing, warmth, sex, sleep.
If these needs are not satisfied the human body cannot function optimally. Maslow considered physiological needs the most important as all the other needs become secondary until these needs are met.
2. **Safety needs** - protection from elements, security, order, law, stability, freedom from fear.
3. **Love and belongingness needs** - after physiological and safety needs have been fulfilled, the third level of human needs is social and involves feelings of belongingness. The need for interpersonal relationships motivates behavior.
Examples include friendship, intimacy, trust, and acceptance, receiving and giving affection and love. Affiliating, being part of a group (family, friends, work).
4. **Esteem needs** - which Maslow classified into two categories: (i) esteem for oneself (dignity, achievement, mastery, independence) and (ii) the desire for reputation or respect from others (e.g., status, prestige).
Maslow indicated that the need for respect or reputation is most important for children and adolescents and precedes real self-esteem or dignity.
5. **Self-actualization needs** - realizing personal potential, self-fulfillment, seeking personal growth and peak experiences. A desire "to become everything one is capable of becoming"(Maslow, 1987, p. 64).

It is helpful, when faced with any behavior, that we consider the function of why the response is happening and how it is reinforcing to the person. When we can identify the needs not being met and the function of the behavior, we understand ourselves and others in a more clear and compassionate way.

In my current position as a school counselor, we are lucky to have two mental health workers including a licensed counselor and a highly skilled social worker. We also have a community liaison, a dedicated assistant principal, and an innovative principal in addition to an amazing special education team and a phenomenal group of teachers and other staff members who support our students and parents. One would think that all of that would be more than enough to meet the needs of 470 students. I mean, with all these resources and the fact that all staff is extensively trained in *Capturing Kids Hearts 1* (CKH), we should be able to do more than just "manage." In April of 2019, Flip Flippen with the Flippen Group named our school as a National Showcase School for CKH. This is an amazing accomplishment considering that the rigorous 3-year process only took our staff 2 years to prove our competency at a national level. *Capturing Kids' Hearts 1* is an immersive, participatory experience. Teachers, staff, and administrators learn and practice skills they will use and model in their classrooms, schools, and districts, including:

- How to build meaningful, productive relationships with every student and every colleague.
- How to use the *EXCEL Model* of teaching to create a safe, effective environment for learning.
- How to develop self-managing, high-performing classrooms using team-building skills and a Social Contract.

- High payoff techniques for dealing with conflict, negative behavior, and disrespect issues.

With this honorary title, a highly competent collaborative staff, a state-recognized district behavior interventionist, multiple skilled academic interventionists, and an amazing administrator, one would expect that our students would likely have minimal difficulties and the teachers would experience little disruption during lessons. In fact, the scenario first described in this chapter is just a fraction of what happens on any given day at our school. Because of this disconnect, it was apparent to our innovative principal that we still needed more tools. This year we implemented, school wide, a free on line curriculum called Random Acts of Kindness (RAK) which is research based and has shown good results, but again still was not enough. We have a group of students so impacted that even another layer of support has been necessary to address the needs of those teachers, students and families. Luckily, Charmas and Janice Lee have come to the rescue and have partnered with our staff and parents to provide the ACE program that incorporates the essential concepts of Think, Say Do. They have not only partnered with us, their dedication and perseverance with the program with our toughest students has modeled how unfailing belief in something can create positive change. This program and approach to self-regulation has been life changing for many of our students and teachers! Don't get me wrong, we are still seeking more tools every day to address the difficulties our students and families face and nothing we have found yet will cure poverty, hunger, incarceration, domestic violence, suicidal ideation, the need for the Department of Human Services, serious mental health diagnoses, learning disabilities, and severe complex or generational trauma, but ACE with the focus on *Think Say Do* does help people to more effectively deal with and navigate overcoming life's simple and complex challenges. We piloted this model with our most needy, severely traumatized and highly impacted kids. **Think Say Do** has become a mantra for many in our building as we navigate difficult situations for both students and staff.

Think Say Do also helps teachers and parents alike. There are many staff who burn out within the first 5 years and give up because of the mental and physical exhaustion. Those who stay with it, truly have a passion for children and an undying desire to truly make a difference in our world today and in the future. In order for anyone to survive in education, and honestly as any caregiver, they must believe in themselves and those that they support. It is true that it takes a village to raise a child and a caring collaborative community to nurture success. We have gladly welcomed Mr. and Mrs. Lee to help us collectively offer support for ourselves and to others. **Think Say Do** has become part of our culture and has already made an amazing lasting impression on those who have had both direct and indirect exposure to the program. One of Coach Lee's missions is to never give up and to capture as many students as possible. Mrs. Lee is always there to reinforce this mission and approach. She literally brings homemade baked goods to genuinely reward students for hard work. She is no nonsense though. If you don't earn it, you don't get it! And let me tell you, the kids WANT what she has to offer! When I think of Mr. and Mrs. Lee I think of The Legend Of The Starfish. There are many versions, but I ask you to contemplate this augmented version of:

The Legend Of The Starfish

There were people walking down a beautiful sandy beach. In the distance, they saw other people who were very intentional and purposeful about every move they made. So focused that they repeated it over and over.

As the group got closer, they saw everyone picking up stranded starfish that had washed up on land. They were frantically throwing each one they could find back into the sea.

The group gazed in wonder as the group, again and again, threw the small starfish from the sand to the water.

They asked, "Hey, why are you all spending so much energy doing what seems to be a BIG waste of time?" There were literally thousands of starfish and only a handful of people trying to help.

Then one of the people explained that the stranded starfish would die if left in the morning sun, and that he would do his best to make a difference.

The one who asked for the explanation said, "But there must be thousands of beaches and millions of starfish! How can any of you really make any difference?"

They looked at the small starfish in hands of each person ready to throw one back into the ocean, and as the starfish were tossed into the safety of the sea, the people confidently exclaimed, ***"It makes a difference to this one!"***

I believe that this legend truly embodies the concept of ***Think Say Do*** in the ACE Program!

- As I think, I become (a change agent for many).
- As I speak, I create (a new reality for the starfish).
- As I Do, I do the work with intention/purpose and enthusiasm (We make a difference for the ***one*** and collectively ***we*** can make a difference for the many).

In essence, what we do, MATTERS! One may argue, that this concept is great in theory, but we can't truly make the difference that this fictitious story implies. The reality sets in about the limits we have, the challenges we face and the barriers that seem insurmountable depending on the circumstance. When we take a step back and apply the simple concept of ***Think Say Do***, things really do begin to change. I have witnessed it myself in amazing ways!

As adults, children depend on us for many things. One of the most important things is to be in control, calm and able to self-regulate when over excited, worried, sad or angry. They watch every non-verbal expression adults use and often mimic the demonstrated attitude, spoken words, tone and actions. In this way, if we can control our response, children will learn self-control and will be able to demonstrate authentic intrinsic fortitude leading to a strong self-esteem and feelings of self-efficacy.

Sadly, according to the book Helping Billy (p.55), The author Heather Forbes states that, "Unfortunately, by the time a child is eight years old, he is typically told seven times more negative messages than positive messages. What is said to children at this vulnerable age does matter, as do the experiences the child has with adults in his life. It molds the very essence of who this child becomes and who he perceives himself to be in the world." When keeping the lasting effects of trauma in mind, many adults suffer from unresolved traumatic experiences. If adults have not processed their own trauma, they can be triggered and that can affect their reaction in specific situations. Ultimately, whether a person is one or one hundred, it is imperative to consider past trauma and take that into account when working with them.

So, what actually is considered trauma? "Trauma is an exceptional experience in which powerful and dangerous events overwhelm a person's capacity to cope" (Rice & Groves, 2005)." In fact, experiences do not need to be life-threatening to trigger a trauma response. The Adverse Childhood Experiences (ACEs) can have significant impact on child development." The ACEs study is described by The Center For The Application Of Prevention Technologies. They identify ACEs as stressful or traumatic events, including abuse and neglect. They may also include household dysfunction such as witnessing domestic violence or growing up with family members who have substance use disorders. ACEs are strongly related to the development and prevalence of a wide range of health problems throughout a person's lifespan, including those associated with substance misuse.

ACEs include:
- Physical abuse
- Sexual abuse
- Emotional abuse
- Physical neglect
- Emotional neglect
- Intimate partner violence
- Mother treated violently

- Substance misuse within household
- Household mental illness
- Parental separation or divorce
- Incarcerated household member

ACEs are a good example of the types of complex issues...The negative effects of ACEs are felt throughout the nation and can affect people of all backgrounds. "Students exposed to trauma and toxic stress are more likely to struggle with academic success. Trauma does not discriminate. It happens across all communities and cultures." (Sours and Hall, p.1)

It has been shown that a person's brain function and structure can literally be altered and a person's estimated life span can be shortened by a person's perception of life's experiences. If an experience is perceived as traumatic, there is a likelihood of significant health problems in later life and the person's life expectancy is decreased significantly. Because of this research, it is imperative that we be sensitive to how people perceive events and if someone is reacting in a manner in which they appear to be seeking attention, we MUST feed the need. We must give them the right kind of attention so they don't have to depend on maladaptive ways to get it. Education staff have many hours in a child's life to influence student brain functioning.

School staff members spend an average of about 45 hours a week with students. This is many times more waking "quality" hours than the identified caregivers spend with them. Because of the extensive exposure to school culture, educators must constantly keep themselves "in check" and be experts at many things. Self-regulating their own emotional responses is at the top of the list. This modeling and calmness can be what literally makes or breaks a child. We can't take that chance; we must be purposeful in what we Think, Say and Do in order to teach our students to do the same.

Thankfully, children's brains are plastic when the right environment is provided. Forbes explains that, "Being supported through a safe, nurturing, and calm relationship with his teacher allows his nervous system the chance to settle down. New neuropathways can be created and old behavioral patterns that have kept him locked in a pattern of acting out can be rewritten...Profound changes and healing can occur." (Forbes, P.20) This is very encouraging, especially when we realize that most of offering a safe nurturing environment primarily depends on our attitude.

Attitude is everything! Neila Connors, from her book, *If You Don't Feed The Teachers They Will Eat The Students*, stresses that, "Everything evolves around one's attitude...You can have a positive attitude without talent and you can have talent without a positive attitude, but things really start happening when you have a positive attitude combined with talent." This is what makes both children and adults successful. Our attitude can influence other's attitudes! Let's make it a positive influence! Conners goes on to say that, "…some people suffer from psycho-sclerosis, which is the hardening of the attitude." (Connors, p.48). They blame their negative attitude on many reasons I hear every day. These include parents not trusting the school or wanting to get involved, the child's home life, another grade level didn't prepare them or concerns that "something" is really wrong with that kid. Realistically, teachers need the support of administration as well as colleagues. There are many ways leaders can help teachers and feed their critical needs so teachers can, in turn, feed the needs of students. (Connors, p.48). I have always believed in feeding the need from my residential and behavior interventionist days. Melvin Konnerk in his book Childhood: A Multicultural View also shares my thoughts. He said, "In order to be treated fairly and equally, children have to be treated differently." Fairness does not mean equality! It means that everyone gets what they need when they need it! In every role I have played in education, I have used this concept and it has made a difference. It is just like the tiny starfish needing to be tossed back into the sea to satisfy a basic need. Not all starfish need to be saved, those already in the water need something different, but they still have needs. The same holds true for all people. It is just the skill to identify what that is and the healthy way to support them getting that need met.

Another universal truth that I have found to be true is that rules without relationships equal rebellion. Whether we are talking about people who have suffered trauma or those that just need a little extra encouragement, without the relationship, we will, as one

3rd grade teacher put it, "Go for a ride on the struggle bus." This made me laugh. It gave me a true vision of what we all experience together. We each have our own struggle bus at different times. Humor is always a recommended tool! It should be mastered early on. I not only use humor in times of struggle, but I look for those things to celebrate. These two things are a part of my conscious self-care plan. Recently, another teacher made me laugh, as well, when she said she tells her students the old Block Buster tag line "Be Kind, Rewind." She uses this when her students do or say something unkind. Little moments to giggle together builds relationships and helps one another keep things in perspective.

We quickly realize that all these things are best practiced when working with children and adults, but if there are things we are not used to doing or if we don't philosophically align with the concept, change is especially hard and tools are more difficult to implement. "The truth is that through any change, 5% of the people will accept it immediately, 25% will slowly adapt and accept, 60% will take a "let's wait and see" approach and will eventually accept the new idea if it works to their advantage, and 10% of people will never accept any change." (Conners, p.47) Part of being a leader in education or a leader as a caregiver and/or a self-reflective individual, is realizing what we can control and what we can't. Sometimes it is time to Think that it is ok to walk away, and Say I can't fix it and Do something different. Keeping those 10% in mind that will refuse to change, we "Don't waste time fertilizing rocks or watering weeds." (Conner, p.47) We spend our energy where we can make a difference. Throwing a starfish that is already dead is not going to bring the starfish back to life. Sometimes we have to let go and move on to the one we can save and realize we can't do it all. We need to rely on others and perhaps they have a skill or tool we have not mastered yet and it is OK for that person to take it from there. The concept of **Think Say Do** can be used when needing to let go and realize that it is OK not to always be OK. Showing empathy for the sad circumstance goes a long way with people and especially children even if you can't offer support for every problem. Being authentic and admitting when we can't or are not willing to do something is just as valuable as offering unwanted or unneeded help.

In all the beginning chaos, sometimes I hear…"Hey, school mom!" from around the corner. Another student's crying is initially recognized after getting into a conflict with peer and quickly begins to taper off as we notice a staff member kneeling to the height of a student to make eye contact. Daily, I see whole grade levels sharing their *good things* as a part of the daily routine from CKH and a 5th grader entering the building excited to be Star Student for the day and lead the pledge in the Great Gathering before school even begins. And often I can see in the background and notice a student in the principal's office sharing what happened in a fight on the playground and the student taking responsibility for actions never owned before. That student then shares what they will choose to do the next time a conflict arises. Lastly, in my office, I am often talking with a student and have the opportunity to say, "I can't wait to tell Coach Lee and Janice how you have used your ACE strategies! Let's call your grandma and you can celebrate telling her what great choices you made today and how you showed you are a true leader!" On a daily basis, we not only the hectic and chaotic, dangerous and threatening words and see things we shutter to admit happen in an elementary school, but we also get to reframe the negative experiences as opportunities to practice weak skills and celebrate those small successes and opportunities to build relationships with children. We get to tell parents all the good things their children did during the day and how we notice they have grown. All of these moments are priceless.

AFTERWORD

I mentioned earlier that life is a process of continuing education. Principles and doctrines mean nothing unless they result in a life changing dynamic. To determine if the **Think Say Do** hypothesis is true-or-not, you will have to apply the strategies, practices, and routines shared in **Think Say Do** thoroughly. Writing **Think Say Do** was quite a journey. I learned many things that I have encapsulated in the nine C's of success below.

Compass

I've learned that most people are not looking for a hero, they are looking for a guide who gets excited every time he sees them recognize their value and is willing to provide them with a compass or blueprint to achieve success. I've learned that you don't have to know all the answers, you have to know who you are and who they are.

Clarity

I've learned to keep the communications simple because *simplicity promotes clarity and clarity accelerates outcomes.*

Complexity

I've learned that no two people are the same, in fact they are *equally different.*

Compromise

I've learned to *compromise on the non-essentials.*

Courage

I've learned that it takes courage to embrace the brutal facts of a *current reality.*

Confidence

I've learned it takes confidence to have *an unwavering faith in the end result.*

Consistency

I've learned that it takes consistency to maintain a sense of *greater expectations within oneself.*

Commitment

I've learned that you must be "*all in*" to make the decision to win.

Collaboration

I've learned that when an individual pushes his limits, he will quickly find them, but through collaborating *a team can MOVE THE EARTH.*

I hope you have enjoyed your journey through **Think Say Do**. It has been my honor to be your coach.

Coaching is the GREATEST Profession in the World!
Charmas B. Lee

REFERENCES

Bompa, T., & Carrera, M. (2005) *Periodization training for sports.* Champaign, IL: Human Kinetics

Burchard, Brendon (2014) The Motivation Manifesto, 9 Declarations to Claim Your Personal Power: Hay House Inc.

Burchard, B. (2017) High Performance Habits, How Extraordinary People Became That Way: Hay House Inc.

Cloud, H. (2013) Boundaries for Leaders, Results Relationships and Being Ridiculously in Charge: New York: Harper Collins

Clear, J. (2018) Atomic Habits, Tiny Changes, Remarkable Results: Penguin Random House

Connors, N.A. (2000). *If you don't feed the teachers they eat the students.* Nashville, Tennessee: Incentive Publication
https://flippengroup.com/education/capturing-kids-hearts-1/

Covey, S. (1989) *The seven habits of highly effective people, powerful lessons in personal change.* New York: Free Press

Dyer, W. (1976) Your Erroneous Ways. New York: Funk and Wagnalls

George, K. (2006) *Coaching into greatness, 4 steps to success in business and life.* Hoboken, NJ: John Wiley & Sons, Inc.

Gibala, Martin J.; Heisz, Jennifer J.; Nelson, Aimee J. (November/December 2018) INTERVAL TRAINING FOR CARDIOMETABOLIC AND BRAIN HEALTH. *ACSM's Health & Fitness Journal.* 22(6):30-34

Hagy, J. (2015) The Art of War Visualized. New York: Workman Publishing Company Inc.

Henschen, K. (2008, Fall). Psychological performance skills. *Coaching Athletics Quarterly.* (3), 20-21.

Konner, M. (1993). *Childhood: A Multicultural View.* New York: Little Brown.

Lawlis, F. (2008) Retraining the Brain, A 45-Day Plan to Conquer Stress and Anxiety. New York: Penguin Books

Leaf, C. (2013). Switch On Your Brain, The key to peak happiness, thinking, and health. Grand Rapids Michigan: Baker Books

Levine, M. (2006). The Price of Privilege. New York: Harper Collins

Loehr, J., & Schwartz, T. (2003) *The power of full engagement, managing energy, not time, is the key to high performance and personal renewal.* New York: The Free Press

Lombardi, V. Jr. (2001) What it Takes to Be #1, Vince Lombardi on Leadership. Mcgraw-Hill

Mack, G. (2001) *Mind gym, an athlete's guide to inner excellence.* New York: McGraw-Hill

Maslow, A. H. (1987). *Motivation and personality (3rd ed.).* Delhi, India: Pearson Education.

https://www.psychologytoday.com/us/blog/hide-and-seek/201205/our-hierarchy-needs

https://www.samhsa.gov/capt/practicing-effective-prevention/prevention-behavioral-health/adverse-childhood-experiences

https://www.simplypsychology.org/maslow.html

Ortberg, J. (2001). If You Want To Walk On The Water You've Got to Get Out Of the Boat. Grand Rapids Michigan: Zondervan

Pierce, S. (2017) Bright Line Eating, The science of Living Happy Thin and Free. Hay House Inc.

Robbins, M. (2017) The 5 Second Rule: The Surprisingly Simple Way to Live, Love, and Speak with Courage. Post Hill Press

Siebold, S. (2009) Secrets of the World Class, Turning Mediocrity into Greatness. Simple Truths

Smith, V.J. (2007) The Richest Man in Town. Simple Truths

Swindoll, Charles (2005) So You Want To Be Like Christ? Eight Essentials To Get You There. W. Publishing Group, a division of Thomas Nelson Inc.

Vernacchia, R., McGuire, R. & Cook, D. (1996) *Coaching mental excellence: "It does matter whether you win or lose..."* Portola Valley, CA: Warde Publishers

Vernacchia, R., & Statler, T. (2005) *The psychology of high-performance track and field.* Mountain View, CA: Track and Field News Press

Walker, B. (2017) Never Pay Retail for College, How Smart Parents Find The Right School For the Right Price. Prussian Press

Wood, C. (2007). *Yardsticks (3rd ed.).* Turners Falls, MA: Northeast Foundation for Children.

http://www.queenofthechannel.com/florence-chadwick

https://www.theatlantic.com/magazine/archive/2017/06/26-miles-above-earth/524508/

ABOUT THE AUTHORS

CHARMAS and JANICE LEE are the co-owners of Building Champions, a business that specializes in performance and achievement, located in Colorado Springs, CO. For more than 16 years Mr. and Mrs. Lee have been challenging individuals to transform their lives through their dynamic brand of introspection, motivation and personal development. They have worked successfully with thousands of individuals in the academic, athletic and business arena using mindset coaching…a high-performance mental mastery model that suggests that life is 5% psychological and 95% physiological, however the 5 controls the 95. Their unique approach to lifelong positive change is cultivated from extensive professional experience building champion athletes at all levels of competition. These insights have been adapted into a comprehensive strategy that improves human productivity. They have worked with countless youth, teams and organizations helping them to achieve unparalleled levels of success. Together they have published 5 books which are currently available on Amazon.com and CharmasLee.com.

PATRICIA DENNARD is the owner of Thrive, PLCC. She has been involved in education for over 24 years, serving and supporting students, staff and parents in many roles. Patricia has been an educational assistant, teacher, counselor, behavior interventionist and administrator. Patricia has worked in residential care settings, in 4 different school districts and provides services as a clinician in her private practice as a Nationally Certified (NCC) Licensed Professional Counselor (LPC) Registered Play Therapist (RPT)and Certified Clinical Trauma Professional (CCTP).

For more information about Building Champions and Charmas and Janice Lee, please visit CharmasLee.com.

Made in the USA
San Bernardino, CA
09 February 2020